JENNIFER LAWRENCE

GIRL ON FIRE

NADIA COHEN

JOHN BLAKE

Published by John Blake Publishing Ltd,
3 Bramber Court, 2 Bramber Road,
London W14 9PB, England

www.johnblakebooks.com

www.facebook.com/johnblakebooks 🅵
twitter.com/jblakebooks 🅴

This edition published in 2016

ISBN: 978 1 78418 974 7

British Library Cataloguing-in-Publication Data:

A catalogue record for this book is available from the British Library.

Design by www.envydesign.co.uk

Printed in Great Britain by CPI Group (UK) Ltd

1 3 5 7 9 10 8 6 4 2

Papers used by John Blake Publishing are natural, recyclable products made
from wood grown in sustainable forests. The manufacturing processes conform
to the environmental regulations of the country of origin.

Every attempt has been made to contact the relevant copyright-holders,
but some were unobtainable. We would be grateful if the appropriate people
could contact us.

CONTENTS

INTRODUCTION

Right now, Jennifer Lawrence is the undisputed Queen of Hollywood. She may have famously stumbled at the Oscars, but when it comes to being universally adored, it seems she could not set a foot wrong if she tried.

With a record-breaking three Oscar nominations, and one triumphant Best Actress win under her belt by the time she reached the age of just twenty-four, Jennifer appears to have the Midas touch – every performance turns to box-office gold and by 2015 she had been named the highest paid actress in the world!

Despite her young age, in just a few years she has soared to become one of the highest-earning actresses in the business, beaten only by women twice her age, with careers stretching back decades. The critics adore her as much as the studio bosses who can guarantee ticket sales will spike whenever her name appears on a film poster.

But what makes this fresh-faced girl from Kentucky so out of the ordinary is her gift for staying so very ordinary! She is pretty but not stunningly beautiful, she is slim and toned but does not have the physical perfection demanded of catwalk models, and most importantly of all she is refreshingly relatable, self-deprecating, silly, and her infectious sense of fun means everyone just wants to hang out with her.

The name Jennifer Lawrence is instantly recognisable around the world and she has a bulging bank balance worth well over $30 million at the time of writing, yet somehow she has not let her superstar status go to her head. She has managed to rise above the usual chaos and excesses that consume most young stars who find fame at an early age, and in the face of it all she remains level-headed and remarkably grounded.

'I don't think she's really changed,' said Francis Lawrence, director of two of the phenomenally successful *Hunger Games* films. 'I've been working on these films for three and a half years now and she's really wonderful. She's an extremely talented person and very warm and fun to be around. Very down to earth, very silly. She's exactly the same now, so, she's fantastic.'

Being catapulted from a rural farming community to the intense glare of the public eye as a naïve teenager could easily have destroyed Jennifer. Many others flung into the same position have fallen at the first hurdle. Suddenly being lavished with more money that she will ever need might have turned her into a typical spoilt brat, rapidly spiralling out of control. All the traps were there just waiting for her to fall into, but so far Jennifer has steered well clear of drugs, tattoos, dangerous boyfriends and all the other downsides of fame that plague so many young stars today.

Countless celebrities have careered off the rails after finding themselves plunged into a strangely isolated and unfamiliar world, surrounded by people agreeing to pander to their every whim, no matter how ridiculous or unsuitable. But by staying close to her family, and making frequent trips back home, Jennifer has managed to avoid it all. Her strict parents and older brothers would soon tell her if she was getting too big for her boots.

Tragic tales of starlets in the grip of addiction, whether drugs, alcohol, cosmetic surgery or diet pills, are sadly all too familiar these days. There are endless reports of young girls crashing their expensive sports cars, tumbling out of nightclubs and flashing too much at the waiting photographers. They fall out of bed and into expensive rehab facilities with alarming regularity.

Against all the odds, Jennifer is not one of those girls, nor is she ever likely to be. She takes her job seriously and is clearly too ambitious to risk losing it all, nor does she feel the need to share too much of herself with the public. For example, she never uses social media sites to upload photos of herself in bikinis, soaking up the sun in exotic locations, and neither does she find it necessary to promote herself by describing her outfits or dinner choices in mind-numbing detail. Indeed, Jennifer lives a rather secluded lifestyle, a world away from the usual excesses of Tinseltown. So while some stars share their every movement, thought and latest purchase via Twitter, Instagram and Facebook, Jennifer prefers to keep a surprisingly low profile, avoiding the pitfalls of social media at all costs.

She drinks and smokes a little, but rarely attends showbiz parties and there appears to be no danger of her claiming 'exhaustion' and checking into rehab anytime soon. Unlike almost all of her Hollywood peer group, Jennifer refuses point-blank to diet in order to conform to the movie industry's preference for preternaturally skinny young girls; instead she openly enjoys indulging in fast food and always appears looking strong rather than frail.

As well as her extraordinary talent as an actress, and her leading lady looks, Jennifer has also won over a vast legion of fans around the world, thanks to her quirky sense of humour and a refreshing willingness to laugh at herself, which sets her apart from almost every other A-lister around today.

Some critics have suggested her goofy personality is an elaborate act to win over audiences, and they are just waiting in the wings for her to let the relentlessly cheerful mask slip, but there are far more people who seem to find her likeable rather than irritating.

In a notoriously tough and unforgiving industry, Jennifer has managed to secure herself superstar status, earning high praise and scores of prestigious accolades the old-fashioned way – through sheer hard work and making some very smart career moves. She launched her career at a time when the film business appeared to be increasingly divided into two kinds of movies: blockbusters and awards bait or, as filmmakers like to call them, 'passion projects'. Somehow Jennifer has defied the expectations of even her fiercest critics and quickly mastered them both.

She is the lead in one of the world's biggest action franchises (*The Hunger Games*) and a major player in another (*X-Men*), ensuring she has fame and wealth to last her a lifetime. But she has not focused on boosting her bank balance at the expense of her art. Her more serious movies all strike box office gold, too. *American Hustle* was a huge hit in 2013, as was her Oscar-winning appearance in *Silver Linings Playbook* the year before that.

As an actress, the camera clearly loves Jennifer, but she also boasts a versatility that astounds audiences and keeps them eager for more. Remember her first Oscar nomination came for the gritty indie drama *Winter's Bone* (2010), in which she played a troubled rural teen with a desperate will to survive against the odds. And despite still being a teenager herself, Jennifer portrayed a real sense of fear and danger that enthralled cinemagoers. Critics praised her skill and intuition, and from that moment on, this newcomer was the one to watch.

But to be a major star today, you need to do more than just sell tickets at the box office. The biggest celebrities on the planet manage to combine massive earning power with the respect of their industry peers, as well as surviving relentless and intrusive tabloid scrutiny.

Although Jennifer cleverly avoids revealing too much personal information about her friendships or love life, she understands that audiences need to connect with her and so when she has to appear on chat shows or the red carpet, she does so with such familiar warmth and good humour that audiences feel they know her.

Modern superstars often have to endure rather strange – and often dysfunctional – relationships with the public because while many out there want to adore them, there are just as many others scrutinising their every move and poring over every word to expose any minor flaw. The most insignificant error could ruin a carefully constructed career, but Jennifer has managed to turn her awkwardness, clumsiness and perfectly ordinary attitudes into her secret weapon.

'I can go about life free as an idiot, because I have no idea what I'm doing,' she once told *The New York Times*.

She has endured humiliation and scandal on a global scale with ease – her horribly embarrassing naked pictures have been seen, shared, ogled and analysed across the globe – and yet it seems that the more the world sees, the more Jennifer manages to just be herself.

When those infamous private photos were stolen from her iCloud storage device in 2014, she could have issued the usual carefully-worded, pre-approved statement, but instead she was honest and very emotional, furiously turning the spotlight around on anyone who dared to look at the pictures, making them feel like criminals.

Dating famous men and working non-stop has made her meaty fodder for the tabloids – Jennifer is snapped every time she leaves the house for dinner or a even a quick trip to the gym – but despite her high profile she somehow manages to keep her private life to herself and carefully chooses men who share the same attitude as her. They too tend to be polite and make appearances when necessary, but avoid the need to share intimate details of their lives with the public. We are unlikely to see pre-arranged photos of Jennifer and her partner at home or on holiday anytime soon. There have been so many occasions when Jennifer might have hidden herself away or lost her temper with dogged paparazzi photographers, but it has yet to happen – instead she always appears professional and highly entertaining. As she makes her rounds of interviews and public appearances, she notoriously pulls silly faces, bulges her eyes, cracks jokes and even photobombs other stars who might be taking themselves a little too seriously for her liking. Everyone seems to lighten up when she is around.

And appearing so very human is making Jennifer very, very popular indeed. With this one, it seems to be a rare case of what you see is exactly what you get.

Right now, it seems, Miss Lawrence can do no wrong.

CHAPTER ONE

JUST A SMALL-TOWN GIRL

In the middle of a hot and sticky August in 1990, in a quiet corner of Kentucky, Karen Koch-Lawrence and her husband, Gary Lawrence, finally completed their family with the happy and healthy arrival of a much-longed-for daughter.

Jennifer Shrader Lawrence was born into a way of life in the southern states that tends to be slower and simpler than the rest of the American rat race. And that is certainly true of the suburbs of Louisville, the city that would shape the heart and mind of the little girl who would grow up to be an Oscar-winning superstar.

The Lawrence family is rightly proud of their heritage, and despite Jennifer's wealth they have never been tempted to move away from the area or abandon their family home for the sake of a sprawling Beverly Hills mansion. The family history dates back to when Kentucky was granted statehood in 1792. And just a few years later the Lawrences played a major part in the American Civil War of 1812, in which many Kentuckians gave their lives in the battle that divided the Confederate States of America and the Union.

The state has since become famous for a huge variety of different things over the years – not least its most profitable export, the Kentucky Fried Chicken fast food chain. On another, more infamous, topic, back in 1888, nine members of the notorious Hatfield family were publicly tried and convicted for a raid on the home of Randall McCoy, which left his children dead, his wife severely beaten, and his home burnt to ash. The two families feuded for over a century, and it was not until 2003 that an official truce was declared.

In the heart of 'Bluegrass Country', Jennifer's hometown was founded by George Rogers Clark and established in 1778. Louisville is one of the oldest cities west of the Appalachian Mountains. Now the city is known not only for hosting the famous Kentucky Derby, but also as being the home of the Louisville Slugger baseball bat company and the Louisville Cardinals. It is also home to other well-known people including Abraham Lincoln and George Clooney.

Jennifer's mother, Karen Koch, was born in Kentucky too, in 1956. Friends say she always seemed to have an entrepreneurial spirit, and after marrying her teenage sweetheart Gary Lawrence, she set up and ran her own successful business running summer camps for children. Gary was born in the same year as Karen, the son of David Lawrence and Doris Shrader, and he was expected to follow in his father's footsteps.

David had enlisted in the United States Navy and served during the Second World War. After returning to Kentucky he ran a pig farm, where Jennifer later recalled him hosting idyllic summer family picnics. Her grandmother Doris, meanwhile, worked as a teacher for the Jefferson County Public School System, and served as the president of the University of Louisville Women's Club. Their son Gary turned out to be nothing like his dad, however, and became a basketball player with the University of Kentucky, and later went on to work as an administrator for the university.

After their wedding Karen devoted her career to running the hugely popular children's camp she set up, called Camp Hi-Ho. Children staying entire summers at the camp would spend their days fishing, swimming, doing arts and crafts and embarking on magical adventures that would stay with them into adulthood. The camp also provided shelter for homeless animals in their pet barn.

Karen and her husband, who by then was running a successful construction and concrete business, had two children – both boys – and while they adored their sons, Ben and Blaine, they would have to wait a further five years before the arrival of a girl. When the daughter they so desperately wanted finally arrived, Jennifer became the first girl to be born into her father's side of the family in fifty years, so there were massive celebrations when she made what would be the first of many public appearances.

Of course it never occurred to Gary or Karen that their precious daughter would grow up to become a global superstar and household name, with more power, money and influence than they ever dreamed possible. They had no idea just how drastically their third child would change their lives before she had even left school.

But life began in the most ordinary way for Jennifer. Just like many other cute little blonde girls, she enjoyed an idyllic childhood in Indian Hills, the unremarkable suburb where she grew up, surrounded by a gang of boys who never treated her any differently just because she happened to have been born a girl.

Karen was so excited to finally have a girl in the family, she said she could not wait to dress her up in frilly frocks, but unfortunately for her Jennifer had no choice but to become a tomboy if she was to have any hope of fitting in with the rest of her sporty family. As well as with all her male cousins, she quickly learnt to play rough and tumble with her two boisterous older brothers, Ben and Blaine.

'Being the youngest and the only girl, I think everyone was so worried about me being a brat that they went in the exact opposite direction of treating me like Cinderella,' she revealed.

'My brothers and I would scream at each other, and we'd be like "I hate you! You're so stupid! You're ugly!"' Jennifer told *InStyle*. 'And then five minutes later it would be, "I love you."'

Although she managed to hold her own against the boys, Jennifer later joked in an interview about how the tables eventually turned, saying: 'I was the little sister. There was nothing I could do. They threw me down the stairs! I thought I was going to die every day. Then, I turned out to be famous, and I talk about them on talk shows. That's perfect karma for me.'

Jennifer enjoyed what was a happy and fairly conventional upbringing. She regularly attended a youth programme at the Lawrence family's local church, Christ Church United Methodist, and much of her free time was spent fishing and horse riding with the brothers she adored – they were always close and years later she would proudly take both of them along to the Oscars, where they beamed with pride as their little sister took to the stage in front of a global audience of billions.

The Lawrence children all loved being outdoors and the three of them spent their long summer holidays at Camp Hi-Ho, roaming free on a farm just fifteen minutes away from their home, where Jennifer was allowed to ride the horses every day. She has since revealed that while her parents may have run successful businesses, they were thrifty and sensible with their cash. To earn her pocket money, Jennifer worked as what she refers to as 'an assistant nurse' at the camp, treating various minor injuries. This part-time job sparked one of her first aspirations: to become a doctor.

Jennifer never played with dolls or hosted tea parties for her toys like other girls; instead she adored horse riding, but since money was tight the family could not afford to splash out on trained horses for the camp, often choosing instead cheaper and more unruly beasts who needed a home. So as a child Jennifer suffered dozens of riding injuries – she even ended up with a deformed tailbone, which she still says looks odd to this day, after being thrown off a horse during one particularly wild ride.

Although the Lawrences were far from rich, at the camp Jennifer was lucky enough to have several horses to call her own, and the first was a pony called Muffin: 'She was cute but she was a mean little bitch,' Jennifer later told *Rolling Stone* magazine. Before long she was given a couple of male horses to care for, called Dan and Brumby, who apparently hated each other and yet, Jennifer recalled, whenever huge storms hit their farm the two animals would huddle together in their barn. Later she owned another female horse which she gave two names – Holly and Brandy – because she could not decide which one she preferred, although she later described the names she chose for her pets as 'so white trash'. She also had three dachshund dogs and a cat named Shadow.

Talking about her passion for horse riding, Jennifer later explained: 'Growing up, I lived fifteen minutes away from a horse farm, and I went there almost every day. My brothers were into fishing, but I was all about the horses.'

And she went on to tell *W* magazine that as a child she took some crazy risks on horseback, without realising the dangers involved: 'You do become more aware of your mortality as you get older. When you're little, you jump on any wild horse. Then you get a little bit older and realise how fragile life is, and you're more careful.'

As well as spending countless hours on horseback, as a child growing up in America's Deep South, Jennifer also loved listening to stories, whether being read for hours from her favourite books, on TV or in the movies. Whenever she travelled with her parents or grandparents, they recalled, she would plead with them to tell her story after story, after story.

'My parents always had to tell me stories, or I was telling stories, reading stories,' she said. Usually she would become completely absorbed in the tales she was told, and it was often the only time hyperactive young Jennifer would be known to go completely silent. She would remember every detail; her family all remember one particular Christmas Day when her grandfather was re-telling a story she already knew well and she suddenly interrupted him to point out that he had forgotten to mention a few specific details she had remembered hearing before when she was very young.

Her memory was as vivid as her imagination. Friends recall a time when travelling on the school bus, Jennifer noticed that the driver didn't stop at the usual drop-off point for some reason. At the time she was deeply engrossed in the novel *Ransom*, and had become so absorbed in the elaborate storyline that she was immediately convinced she too was being kidnapped!

Jennifer was quite the daredevil, and with her imagination going into overdrive, she panicked and immediately started to plan her escape. Without a thought for the consequences she decided to jump out of the back of the fast-moving bus and asked her friends to follow her lead. They agreed, naturally thinking she was joking. But Jennifer lifted the emergency exit handle and risked her life by actually leaping out of the vehicle. No one followed her; they were all too shocked and scared.

Some years later a friend told *MailOnline*: 'The driver wouldn't let us get off at our stop, so Jen said, "Right, if I jump out of the back of the bus will you all follow?"

'Out of nowhere she just lifts up the emergency exit and leaps out. I've never seen anyone run so fast, it was like she took five steps in the air. No one followed her, not one person. It's illegal to do that, as well.'

Miraculously, Jennifer was not hurt but instead of being punished for her daredevil antics, she managed to wriggle her way out of trouble by calling on her acting skills. 'The next day she was supposed to get suspended but instead she told them she had Post Traumatic Stress Disorder over the incident after reading the book, and they ended up giving her a week off homework,' her friend added.

Jennifer said later: 'I have an overactive imagination. I still have the mind of an eleven-year-old.'

The anecdote has gone down in her personal history as one which sums up her particularly zany behaviour. That incident was just one of many examples of Jennifer's hyperactiveness as a child. Her friends also recalled the time she nearly burnt down the family home while messing around with flammable cigarette lighter fluid, which she decided to spray all over a hot barbecue. 'We got in trouble with lighter fluid once,' one of the pals explained. 'We found some by the outdoor grill and we were spraying the lighter fluid and her parents went mad because we almost set the house on fire.'

Since finding fame, her childhood friends have divulged all kinds of information about Jennifer – and even claimed that her boisterous nature meant their local church had to replace the Sunday-school teacher four times because they were unable to control her behaviour!

Friends also revealed how Jennifer decided to open a lemonade stand during one long hot summer holiday, but this was no conventional refreshment stall. She pulled an elaborate prank on the entire neighbourhood: instead of adding sugar to the mix, Jennifer sprinkled the lemonade with salt and pepper and sold it to unsuspecting passers-by. By all accounts she made quite a bit of money and even videotaped the prank.

Looking back now, it seems hardly surprising that she would eventually upgrade her pranks to photobombing Taylor Swift and Sarah Jessica Parker on the red carpet at the Met Ball and the Golden Globes.

As a child Jennifer was always bursting with so much energy that her brothers changed her nickname from Jenny-Lou to Nitro (short for nitroglycerin) because she was incredibly curious about everything around her and never stayed still – as a toddler, she ran instead of walking. She publicly revealed her childhood nickname in an interview with *The Tonight Show*'s Conan O'Brien in November 2013, explaining that it was because she was 'unstoppable and hyper'. It was the first of many nicknames: later she became known as J-Law, J-Lo and Jenny from the Block.

In the same revealing interview, Jennifer added that no calming medication would work on her, and she was still wetting the bed at the age of thirteen, but would go to school the next day and tell everyone about it, convinced it was 'funny and cool'.

She later recalled telling her mother: 'I'd come home and be like, "Everyone is calling me weird," and she's like, "Well, you are weird, but be yourself."'

And in an appearance on the *Late Show With David Letterman* she revealed even more details about her childhood, explaining: 'I was just like a pathological liar when I was a kid. I think I just wanted to one-up somebody. Somebody would be like, "Oh, God, my legs hurt!" I'd be like, "Your legs hurt? I'm getting mine amputated next week!"

'And that's actually how my mother found out. She came to school and somebody was like, "God, that's such a shame about Jennifer's legs!" She had me purge. I had to spill out all of my lies.

'I was like, "I said that Dad drove a barge, and we were millionaires, and you were pregnant, I had to get my legs amputated, and I spayed cats and dogs on the weekends." Now, I can't lie.'

Being the youngest female in the family never prevented her from throwing herself into boisterous games, which usually involved various types of fighting, wrestling and catapult wars in the back garden. She would demand to play outside with a ball while the other girls preferred to bake cookies at pre-school; after a while Jennifer was not allowed to play with some of the girls at all because she was simply too rough.

'I didn't want her to be a diva,' her mother Karen later told *Rolling Stone*. 'I didn't mind if she was girlie as long as she was tough. She didn't mean to hurt them, they were just making cookies and she wanted to play ball.'

When she moved on to Kemmerer Middle School at the age of eleven, Jennifer proved to be naturally very sporty, and preferred being out on the sports fields to being stuck in classrooms, so made sure she joined the school teams for cheerleading, field hockey and softball. With her blonde hair, blue eyes and naturally athletic figure, she appeared from the outside to be the average all-American teenager, but appearances can be deceptive and it later emerged that her experience of formal education had not been a good one. Beneath the surface she was actually deeply troubled and her bright smile hid a dark sadness that worried her parents.

Karen has told how her daughter started out as a curious girl who had a 'bright light' in her, but she seemed to lose that light when she went to school.

Jennifer herself told *The Sun*: 'I changed schools a lot when I was in elementary school because some girls were mean. They were less mean in middle school, because I was doing all right, although this one girl gave me invitations to hand out to her birthday party that I wasn't invited to. But that was fine. I just hocked a loogie [phlegm] on them and threw them in the trash.'

School photos, though, show her looking happy and enjoying life – and she was once dubbed 'most talkative'. She did her best to fit in with the other girls, and just like the others, she was besotted with pop stars, but it was all an act.

She later revealed in a Q&A with Yahoo: 'My teen crush

– Justin Timberlake. '90s Justin Timberlake, though, like *NSYNC Justin Timberlake. I remember when I bought the *NSYNC CD, and I was listening to it, and I was flipping through. Remember how CDs had the pullout picture things? And I was getting so overwhelmed with hormones that I almost threw up.'

Despite appearing quite normal on the outside, Jennifer has since admitted that she suffered from anxiety during those awkward teenage years, and never really felt comfortable in her own skin until she discovered acting. Although she has many happy memories of childhood holidays and outings with her family, Jennifer has confessed that she was always very comfortable at home, but for several years she found it difficult to fit in at school.

She found social events particularly hard to handle. In a deeply personal interview with *The Huffington Post*, she later explained how she hated break times and school trips, and would easily become anxious about attending birthday parties and large gatherings. 'I was a weirdo,' she said, candidly. 'I wasn't smarter than the other kids, that's not why I didn't fit in. I've always just had this weird anxiety. I hated recess. I didn't like field trips. Parties really stressed me out. And I had a very different sense of humour.

'My family went on a cruise and I got a terrible haircut. FYI: never get your hair cut on a cruise. I had, like, this blonde curly 'fro and I walked into the gym the first day back in seventh grade and everyone was staring at me, and for some reason I thought, "I know what I need to do!" And I just started sprinting from one end of the gym to the other, and I thought it was hilarious. But nobody else at that age really did. It was genuinely weird.'

Jennifer felt like an outsider, as if she was somehow different to the other kids, and as a result was sent for therapy in a bid to get to the bottom of her emotional distress. She told *Vogue* magazine, 'I saw a shrink,' adding that she ended up on medication for several years.

Despite getting excellent grades, and being a popular member of various sports teams, Jennifer was miserable and her emotional issues didn't really clear up until she graduated from high school two years early at the age of fifteen – as part of a bargain agreed with her parents to pursue her dream of becoming an actress.

But she remained close to her childhood friends, rather than adopting a newfound showbiz entourage, and never forgot them. As a teenager she struck up a close bond with a local boy called Andy Strunk, who suffered from Down's syndrome, and continued to send him photos and posters long after she left home.

But far from having her sights set on the glitz and glamour of Hollywood at that stage, a younger Jennifer had always insisted that her dream was to become a doctor – even though she had discovered her talent for acting at the age of five when she started reciting lines from Adam Sandler's 1995 movie *Billy Madison*, and began acting out cheerleading sketches from the TV comedy show, *Saturday Night Live*.

Whether she planned it or not, her talent could not be

hidden and she officially started acting when she was just nine years old and was cast as a prostitute from the city of Nineveh in a play about Jonah and the whale at her family's local church. Her mother later told *Rolling Stone* magazine: 'The other girls just stood there with lipstick on, but she came in swinging her booty and strutting her stuff. Our friends said, "We don't know if we should congratulate you or not, because your kid's a great prostitute."'

Jennifer clearly recalls seeing the script for the play, and realising that was the moment she wanted to act. 'I read a script,' she told *Glamour* magazine. 'I wasn't the best student. I got As and Bs, but I remember being in the classroom and looking around and being like, "Oh, all of you get this", and just feeling stupid. And then I read a script, and I just fell in love. I didn't feel stupid anymore. I just found something I was good at.'

She also played Desdemona, the female lead in Shakespeare's play *Othello*, during a semester at the Walden Theatre in Louisville when she was fourteen. Her acting coach, Charlie Sexton, immediately spotted great potential in Jennifer, and described her as 'inquisitive, eager and attentive' in class.

She was also happy to sing in front of audiences back then, although later when she had to sing on the set of *The Hunger Games: Mockingjay – Part 1*, she was so terrified that she broke down and cried. It seemed hard to imagine her fear when it emerged that she actually had a great voice. When she became famous, *CNN* dug up some vintage footage of Jennifer performing in *Othello*, where she sung live on stage and sounded great.

Charlie Sexton described Jennifer as 'precocious and energetic' in those days, adding: 'She had to sing a cappella and that's not easy to do and a lot of kids will shy away from that. It doesn't surprise me that she had the courage to do that because she was determined and unflappable.'

Following her short stint at theatre school, Jennifer's life suddenly took an unexpected turn that would change the course of it for ever. In 2005, fourteen-year-old Jennifer was on a spring break with her mother in New York. They stopped to watch a troupe of breakdancers performing in Union Square.

As she enjoyed the high-energy show, little did Jennifer realise that she herself was also being watched: a talent scout had spotted her in the crowd. By sheer coincidence he happened to be shooting an advertisement for the fashion chain H&M in the same park. He approached Jennifer and Karen holding a Polaroid camera, introduced himself and explained that in his opinion she would make a great model.

When he asked their permission to take a photo of Jennifer, Karen and her daughter were understandably surprised by the out-of-the-blue proposal, but Jennifer was flattered and excited about the opportunity, so they agreed and Karen gave him her phone number.

Jennifer said later that her mother did not find the situation creepy at the time, although afterwards they both realised just how strange such an unexpected incident could have been. It could easily have been a scam or a trap, but fortunately the photographer turned out to be a legitimate scout, and it was not long before modelling agencies were on the phone asking to meet the newcomer. Within days they were bombarding Karen with exciting-sounding requests, inviting Jennifer for interviews, casting calls and auditions.

Several talent agents were so thrilled at meeting Jennifer that they tried to persuade Karen to spend the rest of the summer in Manhattan with her teenage daughter, and although at first she just thought they were being polite, within days Jennifer was completely convinced that it was exactly where she needed to be in order to launch the career she longed for.

Her parents knew nothing of the world of television, films or fashion and so they took a bit of persuading to let Jennifer try her luck in New York. But their headstrong daughter was so sure that she wanted her life to take a different path away from her rural home that she managed to convince them to let her stay on in the city by showing them a local newspaper article about a boy from Kentucky who had made the move and was already starring in a movie called *Little Manhattan*. Ironically, that young boy was Josh Hutcherson who would later become Jennifer's *Hunger Games* co-star and close friend.

Jennifer was determined to get her way, and so she called her brothers, who she knew would find it much easier to see the potential opportunities that lay ahead for her. They agreed to help convince Gary and Karen to let her stay in New York for two months, even though they too had initially been a little sceptical about where it might lead.

'My brothers called my parents and said, "She's been to every football game. She's been to every baseball game. This is her baseball diamond – you guys would do it if it were the World Series. You guys have to do it for her.'"

The Lawrence family was all about sports, not about performing, fashion or modelling – Karen even said that Jennifer would have made a great baseball player – but eventually they agreed to a trial period in the Big Apple. They knew it was a risk, but Jennifer was determined to make it pay off.

Money was tight, and flights between Kentucky and New York did not come cheap, so the family had to take out two mortgages on their home in order to afford for Jennifer to make the move. It was a massive gamble, but Karen later admitted that the light she had seen in her little girl before she started school had returned in full force once she found something that really excited her.

Jennifer was well aware that her parents were making a huge sacrifice in order to allow their only daughter to live her dream, and she was also aware that they had envisioned a far more ordinary life for their little girl – to grow up in their hometown and raise a family. Now she was leaving home much earlier than they had imagined, and Karen was concerned about unscrupulous people taking advantage of her. As a mother, she wanted to be by Jennifer's side as she made her way between auditions and castings, but she was needed back at Camp Hi-Ho since it was the middle of their busy summer period, and it was too expensive and time-consuming for her to keep flying back and forth to Kentucky. But Jennifer would not take no for an answer, and eventually it was agreed that her elder brother Blaine would stay with her in an apartment in Manhattan. (The two siblings are very close and Jennifer stole the show as a stunning bridesmaid at Blaine's wedding in October 2013.) Together they met with an acting coach called Flo Greenberg, and during the initial consultation, Flo was brimming with praise for this new discovery. She later described Jennifer as: 'Brilliantly talented, lovely, versatile and sensitive,' adding, 'She was loaded with genuine talent and her own instincts shone through beautifully.'

And Flo clearly knew a good thing when she saw it for within weeks Jennifer had landed a string of TV commercials and photo shoots, including an advert for MTV's *My Super Sweet 16*, a TV commercial for Burger King and a modelling job for the upmarket American fashion chain Abercrombie & Fitch. For the Abercrombie & Fitch campaign she joined a group of other honed and toned young models throwing a football on a beach. But none of the stylish photos of Jennifer were used in the end. She explained later: 'All the other girls are looking cute, modelling while playing football. And my face is bright red, my nostrils are flared and I'm mid-leap about to take this tackle like, "Rahhrrr!" I'm not even looking at the camera. The other girls were like, "Get her away from me!"'

Since she was still technically a pupil in high school, and therefore required by law to complete her education, Jennifer had no choice but to juggle her acting jobs with home schooling. She hated having to spend long sessions with a private tutor and in order to make up for the lessons she missed, she would sometimes have to spend up to nine hours at a time studying in her room – which she later described as the worst period of her life. It was an ordeal, but she endured the downsides of her new life because she knew it was the only way her parents would allow her to pursue her dream. Her efforts paid off and after taking her exams online, she graduated from full-time education two years early with 3.9 Grade Point Average – almost perfect results. But despite her impressive achievements, college was never on the cards for Jennifer, and at last she was free to focus entirely on her career.

As time went on and she gradually found herself landing more and more paying jobs, Jennifer had to fly out to Los Angeles to meet film studio executives. Rather than finding it an exciting new opportunity, however, she found the sprawling city unfriendly and struggled to get to grips with a second move in just a few short months.

She found it far more difficult to make friends on the West Coast, and missed her old apartment in the Big Apple, where she had only just begun to feel settled. Lacking in much of a social life, she kept herself busy between jobs by babysitting for a nine-year-old in order to pass the time and boost her meagre income.

One of her first booked gigs was a commercial for mobile communications giant Verizon. It was also one of the first instances when she became severely star-struck (as she still does today) when she got to meet Paul Marcarelli, the guy who has since become famous in America for his catchphrase, 'Can you hear me now?' It was a small part, but Jennifer was nothing if not determined and did not have to wait too long for her first big break, which came with a recurring role as Lauren Pearson in three seasons of *The Bill Engvall Show*. The hit comedy series ran on the American television channel TBS between 2007 and 2009, and audiences immediately warmed to Jennifer. It was a lifeline for her, and she later recalled that the cast and crew became like her family since she was so lonely in Los Angeles, and earning a regular salary for the first time meant she could also accept parts she found more interesting and challenging in low-budget indie movies.

Within months of beginning her acting career, a seventeen-year-old Jennifer was awarded the Young Artist Award for being an 'outstanding young performer in a television series', thanks to her role in *The Bill Engvall Show*, and it quickly got her noticed. Before too long she had moved on to other acting gigs, landing herself a variety of small roles in a host of American TV programmes including *Company Town*, *Cold Case*, *Monk*, *Medium*, *Not Another High School Show* and *Garden Party* – an LA-set drama which is unlikely to be remembered for much, except perhaps Jennifer's ill-advised perm in the insignificant supporting role of Tiff.

She worked hard to perfect her craft, and tried to avoid taking roles that she might later regret, and it was during this busy spell that she landed her first feature-film part in the highly acclaimed 2008 movie *The Poker House*. The directorial debut of flop movie *Tank Girl* star Lori Petty hardly seemed like a fertile ground for any novice actress to thrive in, and the garish overacting of Selma Blair as a strung-out prostitute, not to mention Chloë Grace Moretz as her youngest daughter, were considered fairly dire, but Jennifer managed to get across some subtle anguish in her first dramatically testing part, as well as projecting an underage sexual curiosity which some critics likened to Juliette Lewis's excellent performance in *Cape Fear* (1991).

There was even a tough rape scene, which was seen as a brave move for Jennifer at such an early stage in her career. In the harrowing scene, her character is attacked by her mother's pimp, and Jennifer was naturally concerned her own parents would disapprove of the sexually explicit nature of what she was asked to do, given that she was still in her teens. 'I hid the *Poker House* script from my parents so that I could audition for it,' she told *W* magazine. 'By the time I got the part, it was too late: They had to let me do it. During the filming of the rape scene, my mom was there. I was okay with it.

'I was very ballsy at that age – the typical kind of stubbornness that comes with being a teenager. I started out fearless, and now I'm terrified.'

From that moment on, Jennifer never looked back. Audiences could not get enough of her raw and honest performances, and it was clear to critics and industry experts alike that the road to a stellar career in Hollywood lay ahead, and she was on the fast track.

The Poker House led to her being awarded the Los Angeles Film Festival's award for Best Performance in the Narrative Competition. The accolade boosted her profile further and casting directors had her very much in their sights. *The Poker*

House was quickly followed by another well-received role in a movie titled *The Burning Plain*, alongside Kim Basinger, in which she played the younger version of Charlize Theron's character Sylvia – a young woman struggling with her parents' fractured lives. The role brought Jennifer her first serious critical attention, and even a Venice Film Festival award, for her crucial part in what turned out to be a neglected, off-puttingly self-serious melodrama from the writer of *Babel* and *Amores Perros*.

As Kim Basinger's morose daughter, who grows up to become a fiercely miserable Charlize Theron, Jennifer appeared sullen but also managed successfully to keep some mystery in play before making the hideous mistake that would go on to blight her life. For her role in the film, directed by Guillermo Arriaga, she earned herself another trophy, this time it was the Marcello Mastroianni Award for Best Emerging Actor/Actress at the Venice Film Festival.

She took a brief rest from movies to star in a music video for the rock band Parachute, to promote their song, 'The Mess I Made', but before long she was back to film-making, appearing in the Oscar favourite *Winter's Bone*, her breakthrough role, which some critics still consider to be her best performance to date.

Jennifer played the lead, seventeen-year-old Ree Dolly, in this hugely successful hard-hitting drama, which was to become her first chance to carry a whole picture on her shoulders. Her strong performance was praised for being credible and confident. US film critic Roger Ebert gave the film four out of four stars, praising Jennifer's 'hope and courage' while *Rolling Stone* magazine described her performance as 'more than acting, it's a gathering storm'.

Ree was a teen playing surrogate parent in a grim, backwards-looking, drug-fuelled world, a far cry from anything Jennifer had ever known, and yet she proved that she had the skills to get inside a young woman's headspace and intuitively figure out the fight she had to win.

The director, Debra Granik, almost did not cast her as at first she felt that Jennifer was too pretty to play the tough-girl protagonist, but Jennifer wanted the role badly and was not prepared to take no for an answer. Determined to change the director's mind, she convinced her to meet with her in person and took typically unconventional steps to prepare for that first meeting. Jennifer took a red-eye flight from Los Angeles to New York, walked thirteen blocks in sleet and rain and showed up with unwashed hair and a runny nose; she admitted she made herself look 'poor as dirt'. Of course this calculated and highly unusual move paid off, landing her the part of Ree, who lived in the Ozark Mountains, where she cared for her mentally ill mother and two younger siblings.

The movie also starred Vera Farmiga, and both actresses were praised for their portrayal of young women dealing with the drug culture. Farmiga's character was battling addiction, while Jennifer's character was battling the crystal meth addicts of the Ozarks.

To prepare for the role Jennifer had to learn to fight, chop wood and how to carry a gun. On the advice of a close relative back in Kentucky, she spent weeks carrying an empty shotgun everywhere with her because she feared anyone watching the film who knew anything about guns would know within seconds whether or not she had ever held a weapon before. She wanted to feel as if she was truly hunting, not just pretending.

Jennifer won rave reviews for the role, including Peter Travers from *Rolling Stone* who described it as: 'A performance that is more than acting. It's a gathering storm, a roadmap to what's tearing Ree apart.'

The widespread acclaim also won Jennifer her first Academy Award nomination – in 2011 she was short-listed for the Best Actress Oscar. By now it was clear to anyone with even a passing interest in the movie industry that Jennifer was already becoming hot property and would soon be a megastar. It was simply a matter of time.

She went on to land a string of other roles but they came with mixed success. In 2009 Jodie Foster cast her in *The Beaver*, and although her screen time is modest as Anton Yelchin's high-school crush, she managed to make something out of a part that could easily have been forgotten. She convincingly played the coolest and toughest girl in school, and showed an impressive confidence opposite the biggest co-stars she had met so far, who included Mel Gibson.

The movie sparked quite a controversy due to some of its themes – it featured the depressed CEO of a failing toy company on the verge of bankruptcy (Walter Black); to add to his woes he is kicked out of the house by his wife and forced to live in a hotel. Played by Mel Gibson, he finds a puppet of a beaver in a garbage bin and develops an alternate persona, which speaks solely through the puppet, eventually allowing him to bond again with his family and pulling him out of financial doom.

But with its portrayal of dissociative identity disorder and suicide, when the film was rated PG-13, its release was delayed by two years. However, the role led Jennifer to be invited to join the prestigious Academy of Motion Picture Arts and Sciences in June 2011, a select group dedicated to the advancement of the art of film-making.

By the time *The Beaver* was eventually released in 2011 Jennifer had already been nominated for Best Actress for *Winter's Bone*, although on the night she eventually lost out to Natalie Portman, who won for *Black Swan*.

Undaunted by her loss, Jennifer was typically resilient and went on to shoot *Like Crazy* (2011), another smash in which she was reunited with Yelchin, playing a sexy colleague who falls for him when visa issues keep him an ocean apart from his true soulmate. Although a small role, it was lauded as quite special since she had resisted the urge to make her character Samantha any kind of nuisance or unhinged lover. Instead she quietly and tearfully absorbs the obvious truth that her boyfriend's heart is elsewhere, and slips out of the movie with a sad grace.

After that she won a tiny role as Young Zoe in *The Devil You Know*, a botched indie melodrama that was shot and shelved, then opportunistically released in 2013 when Jennifer had already hit the big time. She played the sixteen-year-old version of Rosamund Pike's character, slinking around in flashbacks looking coolly dangerous.

Up next was *House at the End of the Street*, a suburban psycho-thriller directed by former BBC Radio1 DJ Mark Tonderai in 2012. It was considered a huge flop, although once again critics praised Jennifer's performance despite the film's failings. She appeared embarrassed about appearing in such a badly received project and made a joke about the role when she won an award for *American Hustle* from the New York Film Critics Circle in 2013.

In an open letter to the Circle she joked about it, writing: 'The critics have been very kind to me thus far in my career. But I guess I'm not receiving this for *House at the End of the Street*, so you guys must have missed that one, right?'

CHAPTER TWO

HITTING THE BIG TIME

By the time Jennifer had been cast in a handful of big screen roles, industry experts were starting to sit up and take notice, and the usual rounds of gruelling auditions were starting to become little more than a mere formality. So it came as something of a surprise when she was asked to read for the highly coveted role of Bella Swan in the *Twilight* saga as a seventeen-year-old but lost out to Kristen Stewart. Although she was disappointed at the time, Jennifer later admitted she was glad not to have won the part in the teenage vampire movies because it would have stopped her playing Ree in *The Winter's Bone*, widely considered to be the launch role that got her noticed and led to countless lucrative opportunities.

She also auditioned for *Superbad* but did not land that one either; at the time losing what turned out to be Emma Stone's breakout role was considered a major setback, and Jennifer started to privately fear that perhaps she had simply been enjoying beginner's luck. It was around then that producers and casting directors began hinting that she should work on slimming down, and it was suggested to Jennifer that perhaps if she lost a little weight she might have a chance of being selected for better roles.

Furious at the highly personal nature of these demands, Jennifer fired back at them angrily – even going so far as to claim that calling someone fat should be made 'illegal' – and she refused to bow to the superficial and sexist demands that were being made of her by industry bosses. In an interview with US TV host Barbara Walters, Jennifer asked: 'If we're regulating cigarettes and cuss words because of the effect they have on our younger generation, why aren't we regulating things like calling people fat?'

It was the first of many occasions during which Jennifer would display physical and emotional confidence way beyond her years. Thanks to her down-to-earth upbringing, she had never been bothered about her looks or her body, and was determined not to be sucked into the vicious cycle of calorie counting and plastic surgery so popular among women trying to make it big in Hollywood.

But Jennifer did admit that she had a fear of being typecast, as up until this point she had only really been selected for a handful of tough, gritty roles. 'It's easy to get pigeonholed, so I think it's important that when one thing gets really big it's a wise decision to do the opposite,' she told *Teen Vogue*. Although she refused to starve herself for a role, Jennifer understood the need to appear attractive to audiences, and so she chose a surprisingly elegant and sexy dress, a slinky red Calvin Klein, for her first appearance on the Oscars red carpet, and posed for her first risqué photo shoot, which appeared in *GQ* magazine. And she remains convinced that making a series of calculated moves on her part, while remaining relentlessly cheerful and upbeat in every interview and public appearance, helped her swiftly move on to the next opportunity. And it paid off.

It was not long at all before she landed the role of Mystique in *X-Men: First Class* (2011), alongside James McAvoy, Nicholas Hoult and Michael Fassbender, and became close to the entire cast. 'I had a blast,' she told *Teen Vogue*. 'I was living in London for five months, and the whole cast all legitimately love each other. We got addicted to hanging out.'

She played the younger version of the character originally played by Rebecca Romijn in the earlier *X-Men* series. When asked what it had been like preparing for the high-profile role in the action blockbuster, Jennifer told *People* magazine that she had to shape up for the role, and it took seven women every day during the four months of shooting to paint her entire body blue.

'It was two hours a day of weight training and circuits. She's a superhero, and I'm a wimp, so I had to get some muscle. I needed a few layers of airbrushed body paint, five layers of splattered paint and strategically placed scales. The entire process took about eight to ten hours.' Jennifer has likened the strange experience to 'a bizarre sleepover'.

The hours were long and much of the tough action

sequences required of her proved gruelling but Jennifer's hard work paid off. She not only found a boyfriend when she met British actor Nicholas Hoult on set, but shortly after starting work on *X-Men*, Jennifer got the call she had been waiting for.

Her audition with director Gary Ross had gone better than expected: 'I'd never seen an audition that good. Ever,' he told *MTV News*. 'I saw someone who I knew I was going to be watching for decades.'

To her amazement she was told that she had been chosen out of dozens of far better-known actresses to play Katniss Everdeen in the phenomenally successful film adaptation of *The Hunger Games* trilogy. She may have been a fairly new kid on the block, but Jennifer knew how popular the books had been, and it was a pretty safe bet that the films would be huge hits, too.

This was the role that would instantly catapult her to A-list status, and make her a household name around the world. But after witnessing the phenomenal level of fame Kristen Stewart had achieved after landing the part of Bella Swan in *Twilight*, Jennifer was a little wary. She also knew that the fame came hand in hand with relentless press intrusion and intense public scrutiny that would doubtless affect her personal life. Taking it meant she could never be anonymous again. Knowing the risk she was taking, and how it could have a knock-on effect for her family and friends, she was at first understandably apprehensive about accepting the part of Katniss. Although she was a huge fan of the novels by Suzanne Collins, Jennifer was also terrified of how such a huge film franchise might affect her career. She was concerned about being typecast after starring in the *X-Men* action movies, and forever associated with one particular type of warrior character.

She spent three days carefully mulling over all her options, having in-depth discussions with her family, agents and managers, carefully considering every aspect of such a life-changing decision before she cautiously accepted the coveted role of a lifetime. Of course it was to prove a very wise move, but even as she signed the contract, there was no way that Jennifer could possibly have predicted what a huge phenomenon the movies would prove to be, nor how dramatically her life was to change.

She would earn so much money that she never needed to work again and her parents could retire into the lap of luxury – but Jennifer was too ambitious for that and her family did not want her money anyway. The first movie grossed over $408 million worldwide, smashing dozens of records, and prior to its release none of the previous top two hundred box-office hits had been built around a female star.

Many have put the massive global success of the films, which were scripted very closely around the bestselling books of the same name, down to Jennifer's real-life resemblance to her on-screen character, particularly her seemingly very normal nature, which helped audiences identify with her more easily. Like Jennifer, Katniss is an ordinary girl who suddenly becomes very powerful.

In the stories, Katniss is the teen victor from District 12, one of the poorest communities in the fictional world of Panem. She becomes a symbol of the working classes as the rebels begin their assault on the greedy Capitol and President Snow.

Just as Katniss took up the leadership role of the Mockingjay in the film, Jennifer understood that whether she liked it or not, she too had become a role model in her own right, and that girls looked up to her and aspired to be like her. For the first time she had a very devoted fan base, and quickly realised that she had a responsibility to them. 'I'm just an actress, not the leader of anything important, but being a role model is something I knew came with this job and it's something I have to be aware of and I'm happy to do,' she explained to *W* magazine. 'Katniss has strength, she doesn't get insecure. She's a role model.

'People always worry that I'm wrong for the part: I'm usually too young – or, in the case of Katniss, they thought I was too old. I was blonde, and Katniss is brunette. So many problems. There were a lot of things that we just brushed under the rug. I was afraid that Katniss would overwhelm any other character I'd try to do. But I love Katniss, and she didn't take over as much of my life as I thought she would.

'She doesn't have a lot, but she's happy, and she faces death out of love for her family. She doesn't want to be a hero but she becomes a symbol for a revolution, a kind of futuristic Joan of Arc.'

And when asked what she likes best about Katniss, Jennifer explained: 'Katniss is focused on her survival and a revolution, not who is going to be her boyfriend. Hopefully these movies will make young girls feel more powerful, which is the goal.'

The role of a powerful female fighting force was far bigger than Jennifer herself, and whether she liked it or not, it would vault her into worldwide fame and the big earnings league, as fans watched the rule-breaking, quick-thinking Katniss become the reluctant leader of a rebellion.

The *Hunger Games* movies may have been aimed primarily at younger viewers, but Jennifer took them seriously, and approached her preparation for the role with her usual gusto, taking lessons in archery, tree climbing, hand-to-hand and tactical combat, running, parkour (a spectacularly acrobatic style of running, jumping and vaulting around built-up urban areas), pilates and yoga.

The franchise proved a massive money-spinner for the studio as loyal fans snapped up merchandise – the movies were even credited with a huge surge in the popularity of archery! As part of her extreme training for the role Jennifer had to learn rock climbing and hand-to-hand combat. She also trained with a four-time Olympian and archery coach, as in the films, Jennifer's character Katniss is a skilled archer. Her hard work paid off because she can now hit four or five bullseyes out of ten shots.

And she told *Vanity Fair* that the skill had come in useful, saying: 'One time I actually used it for defence. I pulled into my garage and I heard men in my house. And I was like, "I'm not letting them take my stuff." I had just gotten back from training, so I had the bow and arrows in the back of my car. I went to my car and I put this quiver on me and I had my bow and I loaded it and I'm walking up the stairs. And I look, and my patio doors were open, and there were guys working right there, and I was like, "Heyyy, how you doin'?"'

The sport, which had been previously seen as rather unfashionable, was suddenly more in demand than ever.

Archery Australia's chief operating officer Martin Shaw said the popularity had grown enormously among young people. 'Our membership has grown by almost 80 per cent in the last three years, which is quite a phenomenal growth,' he explained.

He added: 'Archery has had a prominent role in a number of TV series and films, such as *The Hunger Games*.'

Following the release of the first film, *The Hunger Games* in 2012, almost overnight Jennifer was propelled on to magazine covers everywhere, photos were plastered on the walls of teenage bedrooms and she found herself shooting right to the top of every casting director's wish list.

The critics adored her as much as the audiences. Tom McCarthy wrote in the *Hollywood Reporter* that Jennifer's portrayal of Katniss Everdeen 'solidified the connection between the novel and the movie due to her ability to accurately portray whatever character she is given with infinite amounts of charisma.'

She was immediately in huge demand for dozens more major roles, and with the weight of a massive global franchise resting primarily on her shoulders, Jennifer had to learn to be just as tough and resilient as Katniss herself when her profile was suddenly boosted sky-high. She no longer had to run key decisions past her mother and instead was forced to surround herself with a team of managers, publicists and stylists who would run every aspect of her personal and professional life. Clothes were chosen and bought for her, her meals were delivered and she travelled by private jet and chauffeur-driven limousine. An A-list star now, her world had changed beyond all recognition.

To her, it was all very strange, as she still felt the same on the inside. 'I always feel like an idiot every time I fly first class because I'm a kid,' she said. 'And I just sit there, and everyone's got their newspapers and they're on the computer and I'm like, "Can I get a colouring book please? Can I get some crayons?"'

The role instantly made her an idol for millions of young girls, something Jennifer has warily accepted. She has gradually come to understand that she needs to be very careful not only about what she says but also who she dates and what she does in her spare time, as vulnerable youngsters would go to great lengths to copy not just her clothes and hairstyle, but every aspect of her behaviour. 'It's not like I go out and get crazy,' Jennifer said. 'But if young people are listening to me I have to be careful about what I'm saying, which is not my strong suit. I'm trying to work on that.

'Sometimes it's frustrating because there can be so much backlash for just saying something silly.'

For the most part, the *Hunger Games* franchise was all about Katniss Everdeen, and director Francis Lawrence has even admitted that he was sometimes hesitant to show what was going on with other characters when Jennifer was not on screen.

'Because the books are so Katniss-centric, and every scene you see and hear and experience is through Katniss' eyes, we have an opportunity to expand outward from her a bit in the movies,' Lawrence explained in an interview with the *Huffington Post*. 'But there's a point at which scenes feel like they don't work.'

He revealed he had deleted a scene from *Mockingjay – Part 1* (the third in the series), showing a conversation between President Snow, who was played by Hollywood veteran Donald Sutherland, and Josh Hutcherson's character Peeta Mellark because Jennifer did not feature. In the scene, President Snow demands that Peeta help put an end to the uprising.

The director added: 'There are scenes like that in this movie as well, and we thought we would be able to cut away to Snow and see him interact with Peeta. But for some reason, because it wasn't directly linked to Katniss, it didn't feel like it worked.

'It just sort of fell on the other side of that balance for us.'

Another reason why the scene was deleted was because it would have messed with the build-up for *Mockingjay – Part 2*. If fans saw Peeta alive and well, then the big dramatic question of his safety would have been answered.

However, the actors concerned revealed that they had been rather disappointed that their scene ended up on the cutting-room floor. 'I love the scene with Peeta,' Donald Sutherland told *HitFix* in 2014. 'It just didn't fit with their paradigm. It wasn't evident when we wrote it, but it was a lovely scene. Just lovely.'

With *Mockingjay – Part 2* due for release at the end of 2015, director Francis Lawrence attended CinemaCon – the official convention of the National Association of Theatre Owners – in April of that year, and gave hints about what audiences could expect from the eagerly anticipated film. As he accepted his Director of the Year award at the convention's Big Screen Achievement Awards, held at Caesar's Palace in Las Vegas, he revealed what was in store for the fourth and final *Hunger Games* movie.

He said: 'Fans can finally see the conclusion of the series. This one finally closes the story out. This is where we see Katniss reignite and she goes to the Capitol. She goes to war.'

While Lawrence refused to divulge any spoilers that could potentially ruin the cinematic experience for fans, he did reveal that he tried to use reality in place of digital effects as much as possible. 'A lot of the things you're going to see in *Mockingjay – Part 2*, a lot of the environments were real,' he said, sharing that the cast shot in Berlin and Paris rather than relying on computer-generated scenery.

'We found some fantastic architecture,' he went on. 'I try to find as much of a real environment as possible. It always helps the actor and helps them sort of connect to what's happening.'

While the *Hunger Games* series was fast coming to a close, the director insisted that he had thoroughly enjoyed working on the franchise with Jennifer: 'It's been really gratifying to be part of these stories. It's not often that you get to be a part of something that has real meaning and real relevance and real themes and ideas that so many people flock to see.

'Doing these last two movies, these are the stories that sort of bring all of the themes and ideas together and it's where the stories all pay off, so it's been a real joy.'

He added that there was one more scene left to shoot, as well as some digital and sound-effect tweaking that needed to occur before it was complete and ready for its cinema debut.

Jennifer has also spoken enthusiastically about how much she enjoyed the months spent filming in Georgia, even though she told *Marie Claire* magazine: 'I have been running around in a sewer.'

But the long hours spent on set away from home meant she forged exceptionally close friendships with her co-stars, especially Josh Hutcherson and Liam Hemsworth. In an appearance on *The Tonight Show* she described a bizarre night out the close-knit trio had enjoyed in a local bar during shooting. It turned out that the bar also hosted an array of senior citizen strippers, and when Jennifer was given a lap dance by an elderly stripper called Little Bo Peep, she had no idea what she was letting herself in for.

Apparently the old woman would not let Jennifer touch her, and stuck her breast in the actress's mouth! Jennifer said she almost took a bath in hydrogen peroxide afterwards, so horrified was she by the raunchy dance act.

Nights like this meant Jennifer, Josh and Liam forged an

unbreakable bond and they vowed to stay friends long after the director had shouted 'Cut!' for the final time.

As the franchise drew to a close and Jennifer moved on to other acting projects and commitments, she admitted that she was happy with the place her character had ended up. 'I loved that Katniss and Gale [played by Liam Hemsworth] have such a rich history, which we've never been able to fully, fully explore to the extent we do in this film,' she explained at the first official launch of *The Hunger Games: Mockingjay – Part 2*. 'Up until now it was always more about Katniss and Peeta. But there are so many complexities to Katniss and Gale and that relationship because before Katniss went into the Games, Gale was the only person who really understood her and knew her, because they grew up together.'

To her immense relief, her fears about being typecast as a tough action heroine proved unfounded as within a month of being offered the role, she was also cast as a character by the name of Tiffany Maxwell in *Silver Linings Playbook* (2012), the adaptation of a novel by Matthew Quick. Jennifer was chosen alongside heart-throb Bradley Cooper and the legendary Robert De Niro, in what would be the start of a long-running and fruitful relationship between the three stars, who had an instant chemistry, which again proved box-office gold.

In the movie Jennifer plays a troubled young woman who has recently lost her husband and her job. Consumed by grief, she moves back in with her parents. But her family – and the rest of their sedate neighbourhood – are horrified to realise she has become an outspoken sex addict who causes them huge embarrassment.

Her parents may have wanted little to do with her, but Tiffany befriends a new neighbour, Pat (played by Bradley Cooper) when he too is forced to return to his parents' home following a bitter marital split. They develop an odd friendship through their shared struggles and bouts of depression, after Tiffany promises to help him win back his wife if he will partner her in a dance competition.

Jennifer said later: 'I'm a terrible dancer. It was so stressful because Bradley was really great. It became more and more of a stressful thing, but it was fun – like, once you actually learn a dance, it's really fun to do.'

Praise for her performance in this quirky role was staggering. She was only twenty-one years old at the time, yet appeared to effortlessly portray a woman dealing with huge emotional problems way beyond her years. Even the fiercest critics heralded the way she appeared both sullen and sultry at the same time, and were impressed by the maturity with which she approached the role.

The part won her another Academy Award nomination for Best Actress in a Leading Role, but despite the frenzy of excitement surrounding her, Jennifer did not have much time to celebrate – she had to return straight back to work as *The Hunger Games: Catching Fire* was just going into production at the same time. If she was distracted by the Oscar circus, Jennifer was too professional to show it, and impressed the cast and crew with her determination and work ethic, preparing herself physically and mentally for this second instalment of the franchise just as seriously as she had for the first.

And it came as no surprise that soon after its release in November 2013, *Catching Fire* became another huge hit, surpassing Marvel's *Iron Man 3* by January 2014 and achieving the highest earnings in the North American box offices, grossing $409.4 million. Once again, much of the movie's success was put down to Jennifer's gutsy and convincing portrayal of Katniss.

She even received a glowing email from the then co-chair of Sony Pictures, Amy Pascal, praising her performance under the direction of Francis Lawrence: 'Just saw catching fire and your performance was enthralling. It's like watching Steve McQueen in *Bullitt* or something … simply mesmerising.

'And I really loved the movie. Francis did a great job. Amy.'

Jennifer of course was delighted by the praise and immediately replied: 'Thank you so much! Wow what a compliment thank you:) I'm sorry I've been so mia [missing in action] didn't have time for emails during the press tour so day after thanksgiving I'm catching up! Thank you for such a sweet note. Hope to see you soon:)

Xo Jen.'

Her latest success in *Silver Linings Playbook* meant Jennifer could now have her pick of whatever roles she chose, but director David O. Russell was not ready to let her go quite yet, and handpicked her to play a character by the name of Rosalyn

Rosenfeld in his next film, *American Hustle* (2013). Reunited with Bradley Cooper, she is the undisputed star of this witty crime drama based on the Federal Bureau of Investigation's involvement in a political corruption scandal that took place in New Jersey during the 1970s. Jennifer's character Rosalyn is the wife of a con artist who goes up against powerbrokers and the mafia.

Jennifer showed her sexy side in a string of plunging vintage gowns, although it later emerged that her desire for Doritos taco chips – and eating them messily between takes – led to the wardrobe department having to replace many of the costumes.

Costume designer Michael Wilkinson said: 'Jennifer Lawrence is a very . . . let's say ... raw and intuitive young lady, and she's not against eating Doritos and snack food in her costume... So we were glad that we had a couple [backups].'

Many critics found fault with various aspects of the film itself, but once again Jennifer's performance was universally lauded and won her widespread acclaim – she became the youngest actress in history to be nominated for Best Supporting Actress by the Screen Actor's Guild, the Critics' Choice Awards and the Golden Globe Awards.

Continuing her lucrative on-screen partnership with Cooper, which crackled with chemistry, almost immediately the pair were cast together again as husband and wife in the film *Serena* (2014), also adapted from a novel, by Ron Rash. Jennifer was drafted into the project to replace Angelina Jolie, who dropped out of the movie, set in the Great Depression era. Although she was not first choice, Jennifer showed her usual enthusiasm as she launched herself into the role of an emotionally unstable woman who learns she can never bear her husband's children, but then discovers that he had an illegitimate son prior to their marriage. As a result, she sets out to murder the boy's mother.

Jennifer had never really experienced bad reviews, but this movie was plagued with harsh critiques and the release was delayed several times until eventually it was decided to avoid cinemas altogether and release the film straight to DVD. Nevertheless, yet again Jennifer's sensitive, mature and nuanced performance won her plaudits, with Robbie Collins of *The Daily Telegraph* suggesting that 'Lawrence comes out of it significantly better than Cooper'.

But there was no time to dwell on this, as she only had a few days to rest before she was straight back into production for the next instalment of the *X-Men* franchise, reprising her role as the blue-skinned mutant Mystique in *X-Men: Days of Future Past* (2014). In this film Professor X, played in his older incarnation by *Star Trek* veteran Patrick Stewart and in the film's past sequences by James McAvoy, comes to the realisation that the creation of 'Sentinels', robots that hunt all mutants and which have an ability to transform themselves to combat any mutant, hinges upon a moment in time when Mystique was apprehended after shooting Bolivar Trask (played by *Game of Thrones* star Peter Dinklage), the dwarf scientist who created the sentinels in the 1970s.

The complex storyline may have only been fully understood by comic book enthusiasts, but Jennifer played a major role as the movie illustrated how Trask Industries acquired Mystique's DNA and discovered the secret of her abilities and powers. Once again, she was at the helm of a huge hit.

Mystique, a shape-shifting mutant fatale in head-to-toe blue body paint, was seen as such an arresting, provocative and boldly sexy characterisation that many critics openly wished that Jennifer had been given more to do in both the X-Men films she has starred in. She manages to appear somewhere between angry and ravenous at all times, and won rave reviews as a surprisingly relatable villainess-to-be caught in a love triangle between Michael Fassbender's Magneto and Nicholas Hoult's Beast.

Jennifer succeeded in giving Mystique an aura of instability that registered emotionally with worldwide audiences, even as she appeared to change into various different guises whilst playing the shapeshifting mutant.

A layer of blue body paint left little to the imagination, but true to form Jennifer took appearing almost naked in front of the cameras – not to mention an army of burly crew members – calmly in her stride. In a 2012 interview with *People* magazine, she said: 'I have no modesty left after *X-Men* – I had blue in places I didn't even know existed. Afterward, I had to go around naked, with scales over my private parts, surrounded by men. That cures you of all inhibition.'

Jennifer also told *Rolling Stone* magazine how she struggled to get her security deposit back from the apartment she rented in Notting Hill, West London, during filming because her blue make-up had stained the bath so badly.

CHAPTER THREE

TROPHY TIME

In her relatively short career, at the time of writing Jennifer has already received well over 200 award nominations and counting by her mid-twenties, which by anyone's standards is a huge accomplishment. She has only been on the scene for a few short years, but from her role as Bill Engvall's teenage daughter to her Academy Award-nominated performance in the hit crime comedy *American Hustle*, she has quickly proved herself to be one of Hollywood's most talented stars, and she has a trophy cabinet to prove it.

For her first television appearance in *The Bill Engvall Show* she won and shared the Outstanding Young Performers in a TV Series Award in 2011 with her co-stars Skyler Gisondo and Graham Patrick Martin, given by the Young Artist Awards. She was also nominated for the Best Performance in a TV

Series (Comedy or Drama) Supporting Young Actress by the same body for the same role.

However, in 2009 she had to say a tearful farewell to her TV family when she started to land big-screen roles. Although she assured them she would be back, for the foreseeable future there is little chance of Jennifer returning to television roles.

She was amazed and honoured to win an award for Outstanding Performance at the Los Angeles Film Festival for the movie *The Poker House*, but she was starting to get used to making gracious acceptance speeches, which was just as well since the accolades were coming thick and fast.

Jennifer was also nominated for Best Performance in a TV Movie, Mini-Series or Special-Leading Young Actress for the same role. The Marcello Mastroianni Award for Emerging Actors, which she won at the Venice Film Festival for *The Burning Plain* (2008), swiftly followed this.

Her break-out lead role in *Winter's Bone* also led to a string of awards, and the beginning of several years during which Jennifer would find herself dominating the red carpet whether she liked it or not – that was the role which led to her first ever Oscar and Golden Globe nominations.

Even her roles in action-movie franchises, which are so often overlooked by critics and awards panels, gained her serious critical recognition and praise. Scream Awards nominated her as Best Fantasy Actress for her role as Mystique/Raven in the movie *X-Men: First Class* in 2011. Teen Choice Awards also nominated Jennifer as Choice Movie Breakout: Female, and together with her *X-Men* co-stars she won the Choice Movie Chemistry category.

And it came as no surprise that her role as Katniss Everdeen also gained her a combined forty awards and nominations – and counting!

Despite all the plaudits, the awards she has piling up and a bulging bank balance, Jennifer has managed to stay remarkably grounded and she admitted to *W Magazine* that she doesn't understand what all the fuss is about. 'I don't have many talents: I'm not a good cook, I can't clean, and I can't sew. The only thing I can do well is shoot a bow – which I learned to do for *The Hunger Games*, and will probably never come in handy – and act.

'Imagine me 100 years ago: I would have been pointless.'

She may be notoriously self-deprecating, but in an appearance on the late-night talk programme, *The Colbert Report*, in 2014, Jennifer admitted that not only has she eaten squirrel chilli, but she has even skinned a squirrel herself to prepare authentically for a particularly demanding scene.

In *Winter's Bone* her character, Ree, had to shoot, and then skin a squirrel and remove the guts to feed her hungry family. In an interview with *Rolling Stone* Jennifer explained that while she would like to say that particular scene was not real for the sake of animal welfare charity PETA, it really did happen. She had been given the choice to fake it, but Jennifer takes her job seriously, and so she insisted on actually gutting the squirrel herself for the scene. Although she gave a convincing performance, the moment the cameras stopped rolling she screamed and claimed she could never eat spaghetti again.

In 2012 Jennifer was thrilled to receive an Academy Award nomination for her outstanding role as Tiffany Maxwell in the critically acclaimed drama *Silver Linings Playbook*. She had almost lost the part to *Gossip Girl* star Blake Lively, but luckily she was chosen for the role that would change her life for ever.

The months following her nomination were a whirlwind as she joined the studio's campaign to scoop the biggest awards on the night. She remained cool and calm through a veritable tsunami of media interviews, press appearances and glitzy parties. The best designers fought to dress her, and she knew the eyes of the world were watching, scrutinising and judging her every move. Anyone who wanted her to trip up had no idea just how precisely their wish was about to come true.

Of course, she did go on to scoop the Best Actress Oscar, in February 2013, having already triumphed at a host of other award ceremonies in the run-up to her big night, including the Golden Globes, Independent Spirit Awards, Screen Actors Guild, Los Angeles Film Critics Association Awards, Central Ohio Film Critics Association, Denver Film Critics Society, IGN Summer Movie Awards, MTV Movie Awards and the People's Choice Awards.

No doubt about it, *Silver Linings Playbook* was clearly a trophy role for Jennifer, thanks to her impressively lively, prickly, damaged and flushed portrait of widowed dance competitor Tiffany. When she signed on to play the part, she had no idea that it would lead to so many awards; she simply saw it as a well-written script and a golden acting opportunity, which she grabbed between her teeth before flinging herself into the tango with typical verve and enthusiasm. There were other nominees, including Jessica Chastain in the lauded military thriller *Zero Dark Thirty*, but from the start Jennifer quickly emerged as the front-runner of the awards season that year, with Hollywood seemingly desperate to crown her as its new darling.

However, it was her now-legendary appearance at the Academy Awards ceremony 2013 that has gone down in showbiz history. Jennifer arrived with her then boyfriend Nicholas Hoult and wowed on the red carpet. Throughout the ceremony she appeared relaxed and composed, but after her name was called by French actor Jean Dujardin – who won an award the previous year for the charming silent cinema homage *The Artist* – she rushed towards the stage and suddenly tripped on the hem of her floor-length white Dior gown, falling up the steps to gasps from the star-studded audience.

The humiliation of ruining a key moment like that, while being watched by a global audience running into the billions, is almost certainly every star's worst nightmare. She may not have looked graceful or dignified when it happened, but Jennifer bravely laughed it off, and even managed to pull herself together sufficiently well to make a joke when she finally reached the microphone. She suggested that the audience were only clapping, cheering and jumping to their feet not because she had won, but because she fell over and they felt sorry for her.

It was a moment that would be replayed, analysed and joked about again and again. Some sceptics even suggested she had stumbled on purpose to make more of a name for herself, but Jennifer never confessed to anything like that.

Afterwards she admitted to being star-struck when she realised that actor Hugh Jackman had actually jumped up to help her from his seat in the front row, but said that at first she had not even noticed him behind her as she struggled to her feet in a bid to retain a shred of dignity.

Later she explained how the pressure surrounding the Oscars could make it an overwhelming experience. 'It's an honour and an overwhelming compliment, but it's also a kind of bizarre thing. All of a sudden you're at these parties and everybody's famous, and you feel like a loser,' she told *W* magazine.

But it later emerged that Jennifer was being supported by friends in high places, and Sony Pictures then co-chair Amy Pascal had emailed her shortly before the glitzy ceremony, saying: 'I hope you have a great weekend and I hope you get all the good things that are coming to you this weekend and forever.

'I'll be there Sunday cheering you on.'

This electronic exchange between Pascal and Jennifer, who uses the nickname Peanutbutt as part of her email address, was later revealed in a widespread leak of thousands of messages hacked from the Sony database.

Despite her triumphant win that night, Jennifer would never be allowed to forget her famous fall. And in an interview with Dior, the French couturier who designed the glamorous white gown she wore on the night, Jennifer recalled that spectacularly embarrassing moment, for which she will always be remembered: 'I do obviously have very special memories of the dress I wore to the Oscars, some fun, some not,' she said, laughing. 'They need to make it more accessible for stairs, in my opinion.'

But beside that one small quip, Jennifer has made it abundantly clear that she adores Dior, and was both amazed and delighted when she was offered a contract to appear in several lucrative advertising campaigns for the French luxury goods label. As part of the deal she almost always wears Dior on the red carpet.

'It feels nice when you're dressed in something beautiful and you feel beautiful,' she said of their exclusive, expensive gowns. 'When you're wearing an outfit you feel really proud of, or a dress you feel really good in, it can be fun, and therefore make you happier.'

Stumbling up the stairs was not the only blunder that Jennifer would be remembered for during that awards season. Already she had stirred up controversy a few weeks earlier when she had accepted her 2013 Golden Globe after beating Meryl Streep, who had been nominated in the same category for *August: Osage County*.

As she took to the stage, Jennifer gazed at her statuette's inscription and blurted out, 'Oh, what does it say? "I beat Meryl!"' Some audience members did not realise that the quip was an innocent nod to a 1996 comedy and claimed to be horrified by her arrogance for she appeared to be mocking the lauded actress for not winning.

But Jennifer defended herself as soon as she had the chance. 'First of all, it's Meryl Streep. You can't offend Meryl Streep,' she later told David Letterman on his show when asked about the misunderstanding soon after the awards ceremony had aired. 'It's never a good idea for me to wing it, but it was a quote from *First Wives Club*,' she added, as she used her segment on *The Late Show* to repent for her sin of apparently mock-dissing Meryl.

Still, Jennifer did not understand how the internet could misinterpret her playful remark, and hit back at the torrent of abuse she had endured. She went on: 'All of a sudden I hate Meryl Streep. Is that what this turned into? I don't like Meryl Streep? As if I had my eyes on getting that girl forever and I was like, "Finally! I knew it would happen one day."'

But given that Streep is one of the most famous celebrities on the planet, it is hardly surprising that Jennifer's words were so widely misinterpreted or taken out of context and exaggerated.

Apparently Meryl's daughter Mamie Gummer was among those who did not get the joke, and she confessed that she had been confused by Jennifer's ill-timed remark.

And actress Lindsay Lohan took to Twitter to vent her protest against what she thought Jennifer's statement had meant, adding that 'no one should mess with a legend such as Meryl Streep'.

However, Jennifer has long been an admirer of the

Hollywood icon and told *Vanity Fair* magazine that she would never insult one of her acting idols: 'Once I'm obsessed with somebody, I'm terrified of them instantly. I'm not scared of them – I'm scared of me and how I will react.

'Like, for instance, one time someone was introducing me to Bill Maher, and I saw Meryl Streep walk into the room, and I literally put my hand right in Bill Maher's face and said, "Not now, Bill!" and I just stared at Meryl Streep. I just creepily stared at her.'

Jennifer has admitted that she often finds it difficult to keep her cool when she comes face to face with other celebrities that she admires, and that often she cannot help behaving like a star-struck fan. Another similar misunderstanding arose in May 2014 when she attended a private party hosted by Armani and *Vanity Fair* during the Cannes Film Festival, and started screaming as she spotted legendary director Alfonso Cuarón.

She approached him and said she was so excited that she broke out her 'rape scream' for him. The remark was overheard and backfired as it caused a stream of outrage from people who accused her of trivialising rape. Celebrity blogger Perez Hilton later declared that even though Jennifer was known for speaking her mind, and may have thought that everything said at the event was private, joking about the subject of rape was inexcusable. According to sources, Cuaron was amused by the incident at the time, and neither he nor Jennifer issued any kind of public reaction to the controversy.

Jennifer often describes herself as 'clumsy' and when it

comes to her verbal blunders and pratfalls, it's not hard to see why.

As she prepared for the Oscars a year after her famous fall, having been nominated a second consecutive year for *American Hustle*, Jennifer was asked if she felt confident. She had clearly not forgotten the disastrous moment that continued to haunt her: 'Ha! Have you not seen my last Oscar moment? I handled myself *so* well! I think it's really unfair to make a person speak in front of the entire world at a moment like that because it is just so overwhelming.

'It was terrifying and what I regret now is not doing what you're supposed to, which is even having a few words, something that you can say, or even some idea if they do call your name.

'Every time my mind went there, I would feel so much anxiety that I couldn't think about it. Then when they called me, I got up on stage and said happy birthday to Emmanuelle Riva from *Amour*, and then I walked off without even thanking David [Lawrence, the director], or Harvey Weinstein [the producer].'

Jennifer has dismissed any suggestion that her off-the-cuff acceptance speech, complete with the staircase stumble, was somehow planned or even charming. 'It looked like I was drunk,' she said to *Deadline*. 'I did learn, though, not to let the dress gather in the front when you walk up the stairs.'

Despite acute embarrassment at the memory, Jennifer made the most of her big night, and one of the first people she saw when she walked into the Governors Ball after picking her Oscar was Wolfgang Puck, but it was she who was star-struck and not the celebrity chef who prepared the food for the lavish after-show party.

'She didn't know who I was,' Puck said later. 'Her publicist said, "That's Wolfgang Puck!" She says, "Oh my God, I eat his canned soup all the time!" I thought that was very funny.'

Puck has been designing the menu for the ball for the past twenty-one years; and usually about 1,500 people attend the soirée, which immediately follows the Oscar telecast in a ballroom next to the Dolby Theatre. But following the lavish feast on offer, Jennifer admitted that she got drunk and was silently rebuked by pop star Miley Cyrus, who caught her throwing up at another of the many Oscars after-parties. Jennifer later told US talk show host Seth Meyers she never usually went to post-ceremony parties, but her best friend Laura Simpson had twisted her arm. 'I'm just so sick of people by that point,' she revealed. 'But this time I was like, "I'm going out". And I puked all over.'

She was outside the home of Madonna's manager, Guy Oseary, at his annual Academy Awards bash when Cyrus caught her out. 'If you get invited, you're like, you know, super-important. I was in such bad condition and I look behind me while I'm puking and Miley Cyrus is there, [looking] like, "Get it together."'

Earlier in the year, Laura Simpson had written about her experience as Jennifer's date at the glitzy parties, complaining about the lack of food on offer at Hollywood events: 'You are STARVING and haven't had any food since breakfast at 9am,' she wrote on Myspace. 'The Academy really needs to spring for more hors d'oeuvres options because now everyone is hammered.' Jennifer herself later revealed that she had tucked into a calorie-laden Philly cheesesteak right before she went to the 2011 Oscars.

And so it was hardly surprising that Jennifer was not looking forward to her next appearance at the Oscars. When asked by *Deadline.com* about whether she was excited about her red carpet preparations for 2014, when she would return to the Oscars to present the Best Actor award, Jennifer joked: 'Exciting? I'm trying to go back to that place where dress fittings seemed exciting. I've had one fitting here in Atlanta and I think I have the final fitting on the day of the awards. So I just hope it fits.'

And in an interview for her Miss Dior campaign, Jennifer confessed that all she really wanted was to wear a dress that she could walk in. But that was not to say that she was unhappy in the previous year's exquisite frothy white gown, which she chose from hundreds of others on offer. 'I saw a picture of it from the runway and it was just the most beautiful dress I think I had ever seen,' she gushed.

And true to form, when she returned to present the Best Actor award to Matthew McConaughey for his role in *Dallas Buyers Club*, the blunders continued, proving that lightning can indeed strike twice.

But at least at the 2014 Oscars Jennifer tripped and fell early, even before the show started – on arrival, as she waved to fans while making her way along the red carpet! She later told *ABC News* correspondent Lara Spencer that it was not her fault as she had stumbled over an orange traffic cone on her way out of the car, despite having prepared by taking her red strapless gown for a test climb up a flight of stairs to avoid a repeat of the previous year's disaster. 'This year I actually did a stair test out on the back staircase and got it a little dusty, but it worked,' she revealed. 'But I did trip over a cone, so I guess I'm not safe.'

She added: 'I'm terrible in heels. I can't walk, and my feet are uncomfortable.'

In video footage that captured the awkward moment, Jennifer could be seen grabbing a woman standing in front of her as she stumbled to the floor. She then laughed it off as she made her way down the carpet.

And host Ellen DeGeneres brought up the infamous stumble during her opening monologue at the 2014 ceremony: 'If you win tonight, I think we should bring you the Oscar,' the comedienne joked.

Jennifer later told *The New York Times*: 'That's how I can go about life free as an idiot: because I have no idea what I'm doing.'

She was again dressed in Dior for the ceremony, after reportedly signing a three-year contract with the luxury fashion house rumoured to be worth between $15 and $20 million. Since 2012 she had been a spokesmodel for the high-end brand and was delighted to be continuing the partnership, which meant she did not have to choose between designers when it came to high-profile events – the deal meant Dior would always dress her, and the gowns would be tailored to fit her curves rather than Jennifer having to cut calories to fit into sample sizes.

She told *W* magazine: 'By the time of the actual Oscars, I was so sick of fittings and trains and corsets and people asking, "What are you going to wear?"

'I had to go on a diet, because at all the parties there's champagne and hors d'oeuvres. I ate so much! I think I wore two Spanx on the night of the awards.'

And although she lost out at the Oscars for her supporting role as Rosalyn in *American Hustle* to *12 Years a Slave* star Lupita Nyong'o, there was no rivalry and the two actresses went on to become good friends. The pair had come face-to-face for the first time at the Screen Actors Guild Awards, and Lupita told the *Late Show*'s David Letterman: 'I met her at the SAG Awards and I turned around and she saw me at the same time I saw her, and she made this huge ridiculous face of shock. And she beat me to it, because had she not reacted like that, that would have been the look on my face!'

When Letterman called Jennifer 'kooky', Lupita defended her new pal, saying: 'That's what makes her so good! I just love the faces she makes!'

But it was Jennifer who won at the Golden Globes and the BAFTAs that year. It was her second BAFTA nomination, and she did not attend the ceremony at Covent Garden's Royal Opera House. The first time she had appeared at the star-studded London awards ceremony, however, Jennifer won British hearts by carrying on the tradition established by Brad

Pitt in 2012, when she blew a kiss for the television audience after she was asked to do so by host Stephen Fry.

When her BAFTA triumph came, she beat Lupita Nyong'o, who was the hot favourite to win, as well as Julia Roberts, who had been nominated for *August: Osage County*, Oprah Winfrey for Lee Daniel's *The Butler*, and Sally Hawkins for her role in *Blue Jasmine*.

But since Jennifer was not there to collect the gong from presenter Leonardo DiCaprio, her *American Hustle* director David O. Russell stepped in to accept the honour. It was the second major awards season event she had to miss as she continued shooting for both *X-Men: Days of Future Past* and the final *Hunger Games* films.

But she told *Deadline.com* that she was completely shocked when she discovered later that she had actually won since by that stage she had forgotten all about her nomination. 'Oh, it was a big surprise,' she said. 'I didn't remember that the BAFTAs were happening that day. I certainly did not think I was going to win one, so I put it out of my mind. So there I was, in the middle of being painted blue, and someone said, "You just won the BAFTA!" And I said, "Oh, go f★★k yourself!" And then it turned out they were serious.'

Luckily she had prepared a few words for her director to read out to the audience gathered in London. Russell had them written down, but had committed her speech to memory, where he thanked her fellow actors, writers and of course himself, on behalf of Jennifer. She had also asked him to convey how much she enjoyed the opportunity to show 'Heartbreak, romance, rebirth, music and life'.

Having been at the helm of two of Jennifer's most successful movies – both *Silver Linings Playbook* and *American Hustle* – David O. Russell offered a unique glimpse into his unconventional approach to movie-making in a subsequent interview with Jon Stewart on *The Daily Show*.

Revealing that he likes to get up close and personal with his troupe of actors, including of course Jennifer and her frequent co-star Bradley Cooper, the director and screenwriter explained he prefers to accompany his cast on set with a small hand-held camera to capture their emotions, rather than sitting behind the crew watching the action unfold on a monitor, like many modern directors.

He said: 'I like to be very close to my actors. I don't like to be sat in what they call video village, which is often 100 yards or more away from the set.

'I like to be close to them. I like them to feel me and me to feel them. I like to shoot with a small camera so I can be there.'

While most directors rely on the skills of teams of camera-men, Russell prefers to actually hold the camera himself. And a remarkable behind-the-scenes still from the shooting of *American Hustle* showed the director sprawled out on the back seat of a car as Jennifer Lawrence and Jack Huston sat in the front. As Jennifer, portraying Rosalyn Rosenfeld, glanced casually over her shoulder, Russell could be seen slumped behind her with a tiny camera and various pieces of equipment surrounding him. And the director explained that part of the reason behind their close bond is that Jennifer loved his somewhat unorthodox approach to filmmaking.

Opening up on his relationship with the Oscar-winning actress and her co-stars Bradley Cooper, Amy Adams and Christian Bale, he added: 'Jennifer got used to it, she liked it a lot.

'Jack Huston, who's sitting with her, plays the man who romances her, so that's the scene they were shooting. It's great when I have an intuitive connection with the actors and they inspire me to write roles for them. I wrote for Jennifer, I wrote for Bradley, I wrote for Christian and Amy.

'I talked to them and said, "Let's create a role that's worthy of you being involved". I'm privileged to have their friendship.'

But *The Daily Show* host Jon Stewart offered a fair amount of ribbing for the somewhat quirky direction method. He joked: 'You look like you are chaperoning a terrible date. You are the director and you look like they are smuggling you into Tijuana.'

But the crew brushed off any criticism for the way the film was made, and fellow nominee Michael Wilkinson, the Australian costumer designer, was among the many who sang Jennifer's praises. Wilkinson told how he and his team went with both vintage and newly made clothes for Jennifer's appearance in Russell's frantic, freewheeling seventies heist flick.

'Jennifer and I had fun with the character,' Wilkinson explained. 'We really wanted there to be something always not quite right about the way she dressed, and for her often to be overdressed, underdressed, not dressed appropriately for a situation, wearing things that really didn't work so well for her body.

'The script is just so wildly vibrant and complex and interesting, and I really wanted to make sure that my costume choices were up to standard,' Wilkinson added at an Oscar nominees' luncheon in Beverly Hills.

'And David really encouraged me to go very deep with my design work and kind of outside of my usual scope and thinking outside the box.'

Perhaps the most memorable outfit Jennifer wore was the very tight white gown in the big casino scene, which exposed more of her body than she usually likes to show. 'The cleavage is extremely plunging,' Wilkinson continued. 'We kind of liked the idea that you know: "Is she going to stay inside the dress? Is she going to, you know?" They had this amazing sense of electricity and danger.'

Thinking outside the box came rather naturally when dressing the unpredictable, off-kilter Rosalyn. Although Jennifer was at least a decade too young for the role of crazy-volatile housewife, as the part had been written, age had never been a problem before and once again she overcame that particular obstacle through the sheer force of her unstoppable talent.

It was lauded as her most unplugged performance, and wild fun to behold, even though some critics felt that the director who would clearly watch her do anything was hugely indulging her. Her wig-out to the Wings' song, 'Live and Let

Die', bafflement over a microwave, and the bathroom bitch–off with Amy Adams have already proved to be greatest-hits moments, in a film which so very nearly won Jennifer a second Oscar for her mantelpiece.

CHAPTER FOUR

THE GOING GETS TOUGH

Jennifer found herself forced to miss out on many of the celebrations enjoyed by the rest of the *American Hustle* cast due to her relentless back-to-back schedule of filming commitments, and David O. Russell has often leapt to her defence when she has been absent. During the filming of *The Hunger Games: Mockingjay – Part 1*, when she was stuck on location in Atlanta after the production endured setbacks because of icy storms, the director revealed how exhausted she was, adding that he was concerned about the intense demands on her time.

Russell commented that the *Hunger Games* bosses were working Jennifer like a slave. He told *Confidenti@l* at the Australian Academy's AACTA Awards: 'I'll tell you what it is about that girl – talk about twelve years of slavery, that's what the franchise is.'

However, he later apologised for his comments since there had been a backlash against him making a joke about slavery, which had been considered poor taste. He told *MailOnline*: 'Clearly, I used a stupid analogy in a poor attempt at humour. I realised it the minute I said it and I am truly sorry.'

But explaining what he had meant by the remark, Russell went on: 'I personally think they should give her a bit of breathing room over there because they're printing money. But she's a very alive person.'

And after her two Oscar nominations, movie mogul Harvey Weinstein, who funded *Silver Linings Playbook*, agreed that Jennifer needed a break after a very hectic few years of back-to-back filming: 'She's going to have a long break for a year where she won't do anything,' he told *The Sun* newspaper. 'It's been non-stop for her and she deserves a rest.

'She signed on to do *Hunger Games* when she was young and wouldn't have realised how much it would dominate her life. But she's a professional and always will be. It's been non-stop for her and she deserves a rest'.

But of course there was little chance of a break in Jennifer's hectic diary, since she was more in demand than ever following her awards. She flew straight back to Atlanta to continue shooting the latest *Hunger Games* instalment, but production was halted in the wake of the sudden death in February 2014 of Philip Seymour Hoffman, who played Plutarch Heavensbee in the dystopian fantasy series.

Just forty-six years of age, he had been due to join the cast on set, but was found on the bathroom floor of his

$10,000-a-month New York apartment by his personal assistant and friend, the playwright David Bar Katz, after he did not show up to pick up his children. Hoffman had recently separated from his long-term partner of fourteen years, the costume designer Mimi O'Donnell, and it quickly emerged that he had died from a drug overdose, leaving behind the couple's children, Cooper, Tallulah and Willa, and an estimated fortune of $35 million.

The extent of his addiction to class-A drugs had not been fully known to his friends, who thought he had beaten his demons. At the age of twenty-two, the star had checked into rehab, battling addictions to alcohol and narcotics, but as far as Jennifer and the rest of the *Hunger Games* cast were aware he had replaced this addiction with an obsessive love of acting. The troubled father of three, who won an Oscar for Best Actor in *Capote* (2005), a film about the author Truman Capote, was known for throwing himself into his work to the point of physical and mental exhaustion. After filming wrapped on *Capote* he promised his partner that he would never become obsessed with another role in quite the same way.

But as a string of successful film offers came along, the party lifestyle took hold once more and he started to take drugs again: 'It was anything I could get my hands on,' he once said. 'I liked it all.'

In the run-up to his untimely death, Seymour Hoffman had succumbed once more and in May 2013 it emerged that he had checked himself in for a detox programme after snorting heroin. Friends thought the ten-day treatment had been successful and he returned to work. But less than a year later he went on a desperate hunt for drugs on the streets around his New York apartment and died of an overdose of a deadly cocktail that included heroin, cocaine, benzodiazepines and amphetamine. It was reported that he had a syringe in his arm and was surrounded by seventy bags of what was believed to be heroin, and twenty used syringes.

According to *The Hollywood Reporter*, the whole cast were on set when news of the tragedy broke, and filming was immediately drawn to a halt as they dealt with their grief.

Seymour Hoffman had been making both of *The Hunger Games: Mockingjay* movies back-to-back in the months leading up to his death, and spent the majority of his time on and off set with the stars and crew of the franchise.

His death came as a devastating blow to them all, and Jennifer was left emotionally distraught. Along with the rest of the cast, she issued a heartfelt statement in tribute. 'Words cannot convey the devastating loss we are all feeling right now,' she said. 'Philip was a wonderful person and an exceptional talent, and our hearts are breaking. Our deepest condolences go out to his family.'

It was understood that Seymour Hoffman had completed almost all of his work on the series' final installment, and had just seven days of filming left. The moviemakers were forced to use CGI technology to finish the last remaining scenes, which the actor had not been able to film.

As he had already finished shooting the first *Mockingjay* film, producers confirmed that they would not be recasting the role, and that the release of the films would not be delayed.

'Philip Seymour Hoffman was a singular talent and one of the most gifted actors of our generation,' production company Lionsgate said in a statement.

'We're very fortunate that he graced our *Hunger Games* family.

'Losing him in his prime is a tragedy, and we send our deepest condolences to Philip's family.'

As a mark of respect, production on the movie was briefly halted while the cast and crew mourned. *Mockingjay* director Francis Lawrence was careful to ease his leading lady back into filming without her co-star. He explained how they began to slowly move forward with the movie, with Jennifer and Liam Hemsworth being the first stars to return to the set in Atlanta, Georgia, within a few days of hearing the sad news.

'We started very small, just one scene with Katniss and Gale [Liam Hemsworth] so there weren't any extras around. It was just the two of them and not long days. We kind of eased everybody back into work. It's a big cast too, so every time somebody who hadn't been around for a while would come back it would bring it all up again.'

Seymour Hoffman played the leader of an underground military facility and former Gamesmaker, who recruited Katniss to help incite the citizens of Panem to take up arms against the autocratic Capitol and end the tyrannical reign of the cruel President Snow (Donald Sutherland).

Francis Lawrence compared the experience of working

with his co-stars, saying: 'It's interesting when you work with somebody like Jen, she doesn't talk about what she does. She just does it. It's all instinctual and I think she even has a hard time talking about it; Phil is a completely different guy.

'He likes to talk about things and he likes to keep talking about it and unlike a lot of other actors who like to talk about it and then nothing changes, he can actually change his performance. The way he would dig at a scene. There's a scene with Phil and Julianne [Moore] and Jeffrey [Wright] sitting at a table [early in the film]. It was fascinating for him to just keep digging and digging, and to see the layers of nuance and subtext that were getting added. You can watch it in a way that's different from a lot of actors because he's talking about it as he does it.

'Between takes, he's asking questions out loud and talking to me or talking to Julianne and you can see it evolve and change. It's amazing to watch.'

Some commentators felt Jennifer had been pushed back to work too soon following the tragedy, and in an interview with *Empire* magazine, she admitted that she was ready for a break: 'It's OK. It's my fault,' she said. 'I get little breaks here and there. But on the last day of *Hunger Games* I'm going to turn my phone off for a year!'

And to add to her stresses, Jennifer found herself caught up in an unexpected legal wrangle when the makers of *American Hustle* were sued for $1 million (£630,000) over a 10-second quote from Jennifer about a microwave. In the film her character, Rosalyn Rosenfeld, sets the 1970s-style oven on fire by using tin foil and in the following rants claims the new-fangled gadget 'takes all of the nutrition out of food'.

'It's not bullshit, I read it in an article by Paul Brodeur,' she tells Irving, her husband (played by Christian Bale).

But Mr Brodeur, a real-life journalist who wrote about the possible radiation hazards of microwaves in the 1970s, said he never made that particular claim. He filed a lawsuit demanding $1 million in damages for defamation, saying the film attributes his name to a scientifically unsupportable statement about 'taking nutrition out of food', *ABC News* reported. The journalist also wanted Atlas Entertainment, Annapurna Productions and Columbia Pictures to remove his name from the film.

He believed a viewer could come away thinking he was incorrect and lacked knowledge about microwave radiation, thus damaging his career (the judge has since denied producers' attempts to strike the lawsuit, meaning it will proceed).

American Hustle was loosely based on the FBI Abscam sting to catch corrupt politicians and businessmen. While Jennifer's performance was widely praised following the film's release in October 2013, it received mixed reviews. But thanks to it's star-studded cast, the film proved a huge hit, raking in well over $250 million worldwide, as well as scores of prestigious awards including ten Oscar nominations. Whilst on the night the film did not actually win in any categories, it was a career step that pushed Jennifer into another level of public and media interest.

CHAPTER FIVE

KEEPING IT REAL

One of the things that make Jennifer so popular is the way she always seems to find time for her army of devoted fans, and rarely considers their requests for selfies and autographs too demanding. But she has also admitted that sometimes it is simply far easier to keep a low profile and travel incognito than attempt to deal with the crowds that engulf her everywhere she goes. 'I have nightmares all the time that I'm walking through a mall and people start surrounding me and there's nowhere I can go,' she told the *Daily Mirror*. 'So sometimes it's easier to call one of my friends and ask them to pick up some bananas for me.'

She was warned that the attention would be intense when she agreed to play Katniss, but still finds it tough to cope with the demands of photographers and fans alike who surge around her every time she makes a public appearance. 'The day the first *Hunger Games* came out was a kind of bizarre day for me because I wasn't famous twenty-four hours earlier,' she recalled. 'I got up to go to the grocery store and all of a sudden there were, like, twenty-five paparazzi following me and there was a three-car pile-up.

'I was really terrified and I went home and locked myself in the house. Then my doorbell rang and all of my friends were there with wine and vodka and the things I needed. They came in and we all just kind of watched TV and had a normal day, so that was nice. But it's important to stay grounded, so I don't know. I'm figuring it out. Or trying to.'

If it were up to her, Jennifer would avoid the limelight altogether, but she is sensible enough to understand that appearances on TV chat shows, premieres, award shows and even on advertising campaigns are actually a crucial part of her job, and her multi-million dollar contracts demand that she does a certain amount of promotion following the release of each new movie. Plus, she is often in line for a share of the profits, so it is in her best interests to ensure the films do well at the box office.

But Jennifer has found it hard to hide how much she loathes doing interviews, either on the red carpet or on television. 'I always had a very clear idea of the type of course I wanted – acting, that's all,' she explained. 'Of course, by contract I must assure a media presence to promote my work. But if I had a choice, you wouldn't hear me express myself except in movies.'

She also revealed just how overwhelming she found the

experience of sudden fame when she bumped into *The Hunger Games* (first movie) director Gary Ross at an event: 'He was asking me what the experience was like,' she told *MTV News*. 'And I just kind of opened up and said, "I feel like a rag doll. I have hair and makeup people coming to my house every day and putting me in new, uncomfortable, weird dresses and expensive shoes, and I just shut down and raise my arms up for them to get the dress on and pout my lips when they need to put the lipstick on."

'And we both started laughing because that's exactly what it's like for Katniss in the Capitol. She was a girl who's all of a sudden introduced to fame. I know what that feels like to have all this flurry around you and feel like, "Oh no, I don't belong here."'

According to her proud grandfather, Colin Koch, Jennifer is not at all keen on the barrage of attention she receives whenever she sets foot outside her front door either. 'Jennifer doesn't like the hype,' he explained. 'She looks like she really enjoys doing TV interviews but she's just a great actress.'

He added that his granddaughter hasn't let fame alter her fun personality: 'She hasn't changed one bit – she is so humble and down to earth.'

Francis Lawrence, who has directed Jennifer in three of the *Hunger Games* films, was equally amazed that his leading lady has managed to stay quite so grounded despite all the attention she gets: 'She's exactly the same girl I met when I signed on.

'But the world has changed around her and become wilder and crazier.

'I've seen it get harder for her to deal with and that's sad to see. But she is really a special girl.'

However, Jennifer herself does feel a little different these days: 'It's difficult not to change when the whole world around me is changing.

'The hard part of the job that comes with the territory is losing a lot of privacy and a lot of control over things that just out of human decency you should have control over.'

Unfortunately, as a result of the intensely personal nature of much of the media attention she has received since being in the public eye, Jennifer has lost a great deal of the trust she once had in people. She was particularly upset when she went to buy a French bulldog in October 2014, and according to *E! News*, although she got on well with the seller and they had friends in common, she was disgusted when she discovered that he had taken secret photos of her to sell on for profit later. 'I didn't realise he was taking pictures of me with his phone, which he later sold online,' she explained. 'I don't want to have to question every person that comes into my life but at the same time I have reason to.

'I don't want to change but people need to stop being such assholes.'

Despite dealing with the occasional betrayal, Jennifer insists than underneath all the glitz and glamour, she is still just the same normal girl from Kentucky that she always was: 'I have perspective because I didn't grow up in this business,' she told German magazine *TV Movie*. 'I didn't become successful until a few years ago and I'm very aware of what the real world is and how much a couch costs. I think about the same things as everyone else. Just the other day I bought Tupperware!

'I just can't understand why people suddenly go nervous when the elevator doors open and they see my face,' she sighed. 'Hey, it's only me!' (Although, of course, Jennifer herself has form for becoming massively overexcited when she meets her own acting heroes!)

Despite being a megastar who is paid millions for every movie, Jennifer still tries to live a modest life regardless of her huge bank balance. She loves a bargain and refuses to pay designer prices for anything, even though she could easily afford them.

'It angers me when they put huge prices on furniture or clothing,' she went on to say. 'A shirt for $150? No thanks!

'I do sometimes fly via private jet though, so no one knows where I am. I love my job and I know I'm lucky. But there are paparazzi everywhere. That's a horrible feeling. I'm not allowed to make any mistakes.

'I realised that whatever I do, at any level, I would lose a part of my private life. For each "everyday" photo published, I generally spent three hours playing cat and mouse with photographers.'

She admits that the definite downside to the widespread acclaim, wealth, awards and attention she has received over the past few years has been the constant tailing and hounding by a pack of ruthless paparazzi photographers who camp outside her home or hotel, waiting for her to make a move.

'I knew the paparazzi were going to be a reality in my life,' she said. 'But I didn't know that I would feel anxiety every time I open my front door, or that being chased by ten men you don't know, or being surrounded, feels invasive and makes me feel scared and gets my adrenaline going every day.'

In 2012 she said she wanted to leave Los Angeles because of the amount of unwanted press attention she was subjected to, and being chased every time she went out. 'I cannot live in Los Angeles anymore,' she told *W* magazine. 'I don't understand how actors can do it. You have no life here. You are followed everywhere. It's not like that anywhere else in the world. I don't want to stay in L.A. and start thinking that's reality, because it's very far from normal. But I still love movies.

'I'm just going to love being in them from Kentucky, or Prague, or somewhere else,' she added, although she has ended up buying a sprawling mansion and putting down roots in Los Angeles since then, as living in the area is essential for an actress of her stature.

And in another interview with *Entertainment Weekly* magazine in 2013, she continued to mock those around her who take the movie business too seriously, saying: 'I'm so aware of all the B.S. [bullshit] that surrounds Hollywood and how everyone gets on this high horse and thinks that they're curing cancer, and it makes me so uncomfortable every time I see it.'

She also told *Vanity Fair* how ridiculous the movie business could appear from the outside: 'Not to sound rude, but [acting] is stupid. Everybody's like, "How can you remain with a level head?" And I'm like, "Why would I ever get cocky? I'm not saving anybody's life. There are doctors who save lives and firemen who run into burning buildings. I'm making movies. It's stupid."

'I was like, "God, I'm going to be that person that everybody hates." Cause it's like, "Hey, here I am!" Like, all the time.'

Despite the constant scrutiny, Jennifer has not really changed from the down-to-earth country girl she always was and she still has a remarkable ability to take a step backwards and be objective about her highly unusual way of life.

When asked by *Glamour* magazine in 2012 how she deals with the fame, she admitted that it could sometimes feel somewhat overwhelming and strange: 'I feel like I'm in the eye of the hurricane right now. I just recently started feeling like I'm insane, and I'm starting to think it's my anxiety over the movie.

'I think it's a bit like, "I'm just cleaning the refrigerator handle. The movie's not coming out. I'm going to clean it spotless, and then my life will not change." It's just scary.

'I feel like I got a ticket to go to another planet and I'm moving there and there's no turning back, and I don't know if I'm going to like that other planet or have friends there. It's daunting.'

In another interview with *The New York Times* she added: 'It gets overwhelming, where I'll cry in my car, but not to the point where I don't want to do what I'm doing.'

Nevertherless, Jennifer is remarkably level-headed about the downsides of the business and does not expect any sympathy for her plight. Indeed she has said many times that she fully understands why people outside of the movie industry do not have a shred of compassion when superstars complain about their privacy being invaded. 'You can say, "This is part of my job and this is going to be a reality of my life,"' she said. 'But what you don't expect is how your body and how your emotions are going to react to it. Nobody wants to help us because it seems like, you know, "Shut up, millionaires!"'

Jennifer certainly does not expect any sympathy, because of the nature of her job. She once said to *Entertainment Weekly*: 'When I meet somebody who actually does something to help other people, like a doctor, or even a financial advisor, that's impressive to me.

'"You can do math? That's amazing!"'

But even though she knows it's all part of the job, when, as recently as 2014, Jennifer found herself checking into a hotel and opening her window to find a 'team of paparazzi' shooting from the pavement directly up into her bedroom, she was horrified. Although she complained to the hotel management, she was told that the photographers could not be moved because technically they were standing on public property, and they were allowed to stay where they were.

She finds the legal loopholes that permit that level of intrusion so uncomfortable that she is determined to try and make changes to the system where she can, and plans to make it a sort of crusade: 'If these laws are going to be in place to protect the press and to protect the paparazzi and to protect the news, then new measures need to be made, because this is an entirely new phenomenon.

'This didn't exist 200 years ago. And my belief, and it's something I am going to work very hard on changing and I hope it changes before I die, is to make it illegal to buy, post or shop a photo that's been obtained illegally.

'I have photographers that jump my fence; if somebody jumps my fence and takes a picture through my window of me naked, that's illegal, but the photos can still be everywhere the next day, and that makes no sense!'

As well as battling persistent photographers, Jennifer also has some very devoted fans who will follow her across the globe and wait for hours just to catch a glimpse of their idol.

Naturally, she feels the pressure of being watched around the clock, but deals with it in a typically matter-of-fact way, saying: 'I have to live with it.

'When I meet young fans I understand them because I was like that too, but it's the real life day-to-day run-ins with people who don't really know how to act that make me feel different. I don't feel any different, but when the elevator doors open and everybody gasps, it's an alienating feeling.

'I love my job but there are difficulties that come with it. But it's a very, very blessed life.'

Jennifer usually enjoys meeting her genuine fans, especially if she knows they have waited a long time for her to make an appearance. But she was forced to flee an autograph-signing session in New York City after fans pushing to the front knocked down a barricade in front of her. She had stopped to greet waiting crowds and sign autographs outside the Ed Sullivan Theater in New York City following her appearance on the *Late Show with David Letterman* in November 2014, but her time outside was suddenly and dramatically cut short after a barrier keeping the crowd contained fell down, prompting her team of security guards to grab the actress and bundle her away. Video footage posted online showed her running to the safety of a waiting car, her burly bodyguards by her side.

Luckily, the encounter didn't put her off appearing on the show, and she returned a few months later, although she was feeling unwell, in January 2014. Jennifer told the audience that she was suffering from various gastrointestinal problems, and went on to complain that she was so cold, she was shivering and sweating. She said: 'Do you ever get so cold that you start sweating? Is that just a gross problem that I have?'

Letterman answered: 'I didn't know it was possible for the human anatomy to behave that way,' and called for an assistant to bring her a wrap. He then snuggled down with her beneath a large pink floral duvet. As he pulled it over their heads, he was heard to say: 'Are they still there? I wish they'd go away.'

The interview hit the headlines after Jennifer unexpectedly admitted that she had soiled her underwear in front of her *Hunger Games* co-star Woody Harrelson. As she discussed suffering from severe stomach pain and admitted fearing she had an ulcer, she blurted out: 'There's only so many times a day you can shit your pants before you have to go to the emergency room.'

With the talk-show host looking obviously horrified by her admission, she added: 'It's pretty clear when you first meet me that I'm a freaking head case and I'm crazy.'

But by this stage in her career, Jennifer was becoming well known for her embarrassing remarks and blunders. Not long after that she was presenting to former US President Bill Clinton and mistakenly called him Gill – she later admitted she had been reading from a prompter and believed she was doing a great job.

And in a televised interview with Conan O'Brien, Jennifer admitted that if she were not an actress she would be a hotel maid as she loves to clean and would go through everyone's things: 'I'm a big snoop,' she confessed, adding that she takes pictures of fancy soap products in stores.

And when Conan asked if she worried that people would snoop on her when she stays in hotels, Jennifer revealed that as a joke a friend once bought her 'a ton of butt plugs'. Although she put them under the bed at the hotel, when she returned the maid had found them and put them all on display in the room. 'I wanted to leave the maid a note saying there weren't mine,' she laughed.

Jennifer has admitted that often she says too much during interviews because she is not afraid to express her true opinions.

On *Jimmy Kimmel Live* she stunned the audience by recounting an anecdote about her breasts, saying: 'I just went to the doctor today. I got a chest X-ray of my lungs and discovered that my breasts are uneven. I was standing there with these doctors and they're like, looking at my lungs, and it felt like an elephant in the room. And I was like, "Are my breasts uneven?" And they were just kind of stifled and uncomfortable, obviously. And so I kept thinking, "Well, I'm gonna dig myself out of this hole by bringing it up again." So he was like, "Alright, well, our radiologist will get back to you about, you know, your lungs." And I was like, "And my breasts." And he was like, "Well, bye."'

But Jennifer rarely regrets sharing her stories, however personal or embarrassing they might be. 'If you're having conversations with people, you don't want them to remember you as the girl with the tits,' she told the *Telegraph*. 'You want them to pay attention to what you're saying.'

And she revealed in *Interview* magazine: 'I picked up an issue of *Cosmopolitan* the other day that had tips for job interviews, because I was like, "I need to get better at interviews."

'The article was basically about how to get someone not to hate you in twenty minutes. Every single thing they told you not to do, I was like, "I do that every day."'

As she had shown when she made that ill-judged remark about beating Meryl Streep to scoop a prestigious award, Jennifer herself gets as star-struck as the rest of us. She was even too embarrassed to look at *Homeland* star Damian Lewis when she bumped into him at a red-carpet event, and was reduced to giggles after they were introduced.

She has also admitted to following hunk actor John Stamos around a party, 'like a perverted guy, checking out his ass'.

And while on the set for *X-Men: Days of Future Past* Jennifer was thrilled to meet another of her idols – since she is a huge *Game of Thrones* fan, she freaked out when meeting Peter Dinklage. She told *Empire* magazine that she lost her mind thinking about his character, Tyrion Lannister, and so when she saw him she wanted to fall to her knees and address him as they do in the show, as 'My liege...'

She said that everyone on set was just as excited, especially when Dinklage walked past, chatting on his mobile phone, and they all said, 'Oh my God, Tyrion Lannister is talking on a cellphone!'

Jennifer went on to tell *Vanity Fair* that although it might sound rather unlikely, she was 'in love' with sixty-seven-year-old *Curb Your Enthusiasm* star and *Seinfeld* co-creator Larry David. 'I have been for a really long time,' she said. 'I worship Woody Allen, but I don't feel it below the belt the way I do for Larry David.'

And he responded to her attentions, telling David Remnick at the *New Yorker* Festival that he was 'flattered' by her surprise crush on him. 'It's a shame that I'm about forty years older than she is,' he said.

'Maybe she's referring to her knees [as below the belt],' David joked. 'I don't think I could do it. On one hand it's very flattering and on another hand, it's kind of a shame in terms of timing.

'I'd have fun watching the reality show of it, though,' he added.

Actress Rosie Perez also weighed in, saying she understood Jennifer's unexpected lust for the funnyman. 'He's odd, he's weird, he's crochety, he's all those things and I love him,' Rosie declared, before adding that she was shocked when she first heard what Jennifer had said. 'Sorry, Larry, but when I first heard that I was like, "Are you kidding? Really? Come on, have you seen the man?" And then now that I'm working with him, I'm getting those same sensations that Jennifer Lawrence is having.

'You get it because he's a man who knows who he is, and that's powerful and that's attractive, and he's funny and he's intelligent. And he's also – I know he's going to hate me saying this – he's a teddy bear.

'He's sweet and he's kind and he's generous and he doesn't want anyone to know that, though.'

Jennifer has also recalled to *Vanity Fair* the first time she met pop power couple, rapper Jay-Z and singer Beyoncé, and how she was struck down with nerves because she likes them both so much: 'Destiny's Child was my first CD.' she said. 'I met Jay-Z and I was so embarrassed because you could see my knees bouncing. He was like, "Are you okay?" And I was like, "Yeah, sure, bye." I mean they're king and queen of America, or of music. And then Brad and Angelina are king and queen of movies, I think.

'I've got to stop meeting people that I really love because I just make a fool of myself.

'There are so many people that I just haven't met. I saw Bill Murray once, and I was like, "I can't even get started."'

She has mentioned many more actors she has crushes on, but when asked who she most admired she had difficulty narrowing it down: 'When I was young, I actually saw *The Last Picture Show*, and it was Jeff Bridges, but then there was also, like, Kirk Cameron from *Growing Pains* and the Lawrence brothers [Joey, Matthew, and Andrew].'

She also sent Taylor Swift a text message following her performance at the Country Music Awards 2013 that was 'about six inches long'.

Jennifer is a die-hard fan of reality television shows too. She said: 'Maybe my favourite is *Dance Moms*, but I do love my *Real Housewives*. But there's also – there's *Doomsday Preppers*. *Hoarders* is OK. I find it gets a little boring after a while, but it's great.

'I love *Intervention*, *New York Housewives* – and *Beverly Hills*, *New Jersey*, and *Atlanta Housewives*. I mean, I love them all, but *Miami* – oh, my God! *Miami* is really special.'

In an interview with talk-show host Jay Leno she told how she crashed her car while on location in Georgia because she thought she saw child pageant star Honey Boo Boo. She had spotted a 'breast cancer parade' and thought she saw the name Boo Boo painted on a float, and she was so excited at seeing Alana 'Honey Boo Boo' Thompson, star of *Toddlers and Tiaras*, that she ended up rear-ending the car in front of her.

It turned out that the float actually said 'Boobs'.

Jennifer made the rather surprising confession that in her spare time she likes to watch episodes of *E!*'s hit show *Keeping Up With The Kardashians*: 'I was watching the Kardashian girl getting divorced, and that's a tragedy for anyone,' she previously told *Parade*.

'The Kardashians were just in Thailand, so that was a pretty big deal,' she explained in an interview. 'I'm catching up on all the *Real Housewives of Beverly Hills*. The *Beverly Hills* women have gotten a lot crazier lately. I thought there was no beating *Atlanta* or *New Jersey*.

'I'm trying to stay up to speed on all the pointless gossip that goes on in Hollywood. To be honest, I don't really leave my house a lot.

'I have to find a life that isn't work. But I suck at everything, I'm not good at anything else!'

As a result of her devotion to the show, Jennifer is a huge fan of reality TV star Kim Kardashian, who told *E!* how excited the actress was when they met: 'I was in NYC and I ran into Jennifer Lawrence. We said "Hi" and walked into the elevator and as the doors were closing she screamed across the lobby, "I love your show!" We were laughing so hard.'

And the appreciation appears to be entirely mutual for when Kim's half-sister Kendall Jenner was asked who she would like to see portraying her in a film about the famous family, she replied: 'Jennifer Lawrence, because I am obsessed with her and I think she is the funniest person on planet Earth.'

Jennifer has never hidden her love for reality TV, and told *Marie Claire South Africa* how she indulges in binge-watching sessions when she gets time to herself, admitting: 'After it's eleven, I'm like, "Don't these kids ever get tired?" When I'm out, I think about my couch. Like, "It would be awesome to be on it right now. I bet there's an episode of *Dance Moms* on. Am I missing a new episode of *Keeping Up With the Kardashians*?"

'I'm just stressed by the idea of missing them. Reality TV is my silver lining. At the end of the day there's probably nothing that makes me feel better than junk food and reality TV.

'*MTV* sometimes plays them for, like, three hours,' she added. 'And that will just turn into my morning. Like, I'll cancel shit.'

And Jennifer is not the only award-winning serious actor to admit to a trash TV addiction. In 2015, she quizzed *Theory of Everything* actor Eddie Redmayne on his favourite shows, for *Interview* magazine, and discovered that they have a lot in common: 'I come home from trying to pretend to know about astronomy and physics all day and turn on *The Real Housewives*,' he admitted to Jennifer.

'I've been a closet lover of faux-reality TV since *The Hills*. It's bad.'

'I feel like I'm going to cry,' she responded. 'We're making a breakthrough.'

She then went on to tell Eddie about visiting *Real Housewives of Beverly Hills* star Lisa Vanderpump's restaurant, Pump. 'I went to Pump the other night to meet Lisa Vanderpump,' she revealed. 'I had her sign a bottle of vodka, and when she gave it to my friend who was with me at the Oscars, my friend said, "Jennifer, this is so much better than the Oscars!" We took so many pictures with her.'

Jennifer, a self-proclaimed *Housewives* fan, visited the LA restaurant unannounced and according to a source did not have a reservation.

'When Lisa found out Jennifer was seated [unknowingly] outside on the patio, she graciously gave up her table and pink chair in the centre of the garden to Jennifer and her girlfriends, even though her dinner had just arrived,' the source told *Us Weekly*.

'The whole group was ecstatic because they are all fans of *RHOBH*,' the insider added. 'Lisa sent over complimentary bottles of her LVP Sangria and Vodka and even signed a bottle for Jennifer's friend.' Jennifer and her friends took photos with Lisa, her husband Ken and famous dog Giggy, captioning the images, 'Team Lisa'. Another source told *Us Weekly* that the Oscar winner was sipping on Pumptini cocktails all night long.

And although she has millions of fans of her own, Jennifer tries not to let the constant flattery, praise and publicity go to her head: 'I don't really absorb any of that stuff because I don't think it would be good for me,' she said. 'I love acting so I just show up for work and I film movies and I have to promote them, and then I go home. And that's about it.'

Her adulation comes in many forms. While her *Hunger Games* character Katniss Everdeen may have twice survived the terrors of the bloodthirsty Arena in Panem, she herself has had to endure endless selfies with feverish fans. And it is not just the real-life Jennifer either – she has been bombarded with photo requests since making her debut at the famous Madame Tussauds Waxwork Museum in London.

The full-size wax model of Jennifer Lawrence in costume as District 12's most famous daughter arrived to coincide with the third *Hunger Games* movie *Mockingjay – Part 1*'s release in UK cinemas in November 2014. The model was created in partnership with the studio behind the blockbuster science fiction saga.

'We are hugely excited to have worked with Lionsgate

to launch a Katniss wax figure following *The Hunger Games: Mockingjay – Part 1*,' said a spokesperson for Madame Tussauds. 'The figure is in its own film-specific backdrop, allowing our guests to get up close to Katniss and the beloved story of *The Hunger Games*, which we know they'll love.'

Wearing her The Hunger Games: *Catching Fire* costume, complete with bow and quiver, Katniss became the latest icon to join the Madame Tussauds line-up, following the Benedict Cumberbatch wax figure revealed a month earlier. Further models of Jennifer as Everdeen were expected to be introduced at Madame Tussauds' New York and Los Angeles sites.

Her hugely popular fictional character has inspired many extreme acts of devotion, including a woman winning a gold award at a national baking competition by entering a life-sized Jennifer Lawrence cake. Lara Clarke, from Walsall, won the award at the Cake International contest with her 5ft 10in creation. Ms Clarke had previously triumphed at the contest with a life-sized Johnny Depp cake, which made headlines around the world.

She said she found her second consecutive success 'hugely exciting'.

Ms Clarke spent two and a half months working on the cakes ahead of the competition at Birmingham's National Exhibition Centre, and the Jennifer Lawrence sponge cake required 150 eggs, 10kg flour and 10kg butter.

When asked what she planned to enter next year, Clarke said she would need a 'long lie down' before she decided.

By this stage Jennifer was starting to get used to some of the more unusual acts of devotion carried out by her army of fans. In April 2015 an artist called Mateo Blanco created a unique portrait of the actress made out of 9,658 Planters peanuts. Commissioned by the Ripley Entertainment Corp in Orlando, Florida, the artwork measures 55 x 55 inches and took Blanco 400 hours to complete.

'I love peanuts, so as soon as I began I ate, like, three or four peanuts for every one peanut I put in the portrait,' he explained.

Ripley's gave him two instructions: that the image must represent a Kentuckian and it must be baseball-related. Jennifer is from Louisville and peanuts are a popular snack at baseball games. Blanco glued the piece together, nut by nut, onto wooden boards.

The finished product was displayed in Ripley's baseball-themed exhibit at the Louisville Slugger Museum, and the portrait was expected to travel around various ballparks to promote the display.

'Mateo and his art are bigger than life,' said Edward Mayer, Ripley's vice president of exhibits and archives. 'I truly had no idea what he could create to fill our criteria of having to be made from something associated with baseball. The end result is one of the most original pieces in our vast collection of unbelievable art.'

The peanut portrait of Jennifer was Blanco's tenth piece for Ripley's. Previous weird and wonderful works have been made of dog hair, sugar and balls of wool.

Meanwhile, a Californian artist called Noel Cruz also made headlines with his customised Katniss Everdeen doll, which fetched $2,500 on eBay.

Cruz, who is known for turning mass-produced figurines into lifelike one-of-a-kind creations, said he spent almost three straight days on this particular doll.

'It was a gruelling stretch,' he told the *Daily News*.

To modify the original Mattel doll he had to scale down the hair plugs, before going to work on the facial features, stripping the paint so he could change the shape of her eyes and adding other details with a tiny brush.

Eighteen bids were placed on the final product after it was listed on eBay.

While Katniss did sell it for a pretty penny, it is far from his biggest sale. A collector once paid $5,100 for an upgraded doll of *Charlie's Angel* star Kate Jackson. And Cruz said he would be making more dolls to resemble Jennifer.

'I'm thinking of commissioning someone to do the outfits,' he revealed. 'Maybe I will do one of her wearing the wedding dress from *Catching Fire*.

'I don't want to disappoint the fans out there,' he continued, adding that it was a collector in the UK who placed the winning bid for the doll.

Another artist, David Lopera, designed a digitally edited plus-sized portrait of Jennifer, which went viral. He hit the headlines in February 2015 when he insisted that the actress, like all his subjects, looks better with more weight on her.

He sells his altered images of stars, including Katy Perry,

Mila Kunis and even *Frozen*'s Princess Elsa, to men who prefer their women a little plumper. 'Men are always writing to me asking if I can make their celebrities crushes look a bit fatter,' the artist from Menorca revealed. 'Jennifer Lawrence and Kim Kardashian are some of the most popular requests I get.

'These women look much better when they're overweight,' he added. 'Look at my pictures and you will see that big is beautiful. For example, Mila Kunis is much sexier with chunky thighs and a bulging belly that hangs around her waist.'

The artist has been playing around with Photoshop since he was at school. However, he only began this unusual money-making scheme after his altered image of Katy Perry went viral in 2014.

Lopera said: 'I love Katy Perry but she would look much more sexy with a few extra pounds. So for my own pleasure, I manipulated her first album cover to make her look a bit chubby.

'I uploaded it online and soon, men were messaging me with requests to Photoshop other stars to look flabby.'

A computer technician by day, he has since received more than 200 requests from men and women all over the world. Each work takes several days to complete.

'Usually each manipulation takes a few days but there have been times when I've spent a whole week on just one,' he added. Part of the reason for the lengthy production time is that clients have very specific ideas about how they want the final result to look.

'I know my clients want their fat celebs to look as realistic as possible,' he explained. 'Some even have an idea of how much they want them to weigh. I don't stop until they look perfectly plump.'

Other extreme acts of adoration towards Jennifer have included that made by make-up artist Paolo Ballesteros, who managed to transform himself into an uncannily accurate version of his idol, using only eyeliner and contouring. After adding a hairpiece, Ballesteros was a dead ringer for the actress.

He explained how he basically just drew a portrait of Jennifer over his own face, and it stuck like that (apparently the nose is always the most difficult part). In an interview with the *Huffington Post*, Ballesteros explained: 'My nose is smaller and shorter [than most celebrities]. It took me a while to figure out how to do it. By drawing new nostrils, it made my nose more pointy or bigger.'

He has also found fame thanks to his impressions of Kim Kardashian, Angelina Jolie and Michelle Obama, and has become a huge TV star in the Philippines.

Luckily, Jennifer remains unfazed by any of this and takes it all calmly in her stride as she becomes used to all kinds of unusual accolades. On National Beer Day, an unofficial US holiday, in April 2015, she topped the list of famous women that people would most like to have a beer with. The poll, which received more than 77,600 votes, asked voters not to focus on looks, but instead to consider various criteria when choosing their favourite celebrities, including those you would have the best conversation with, their likeability, things you would have in common, whether they had a fun personality, who was most down to earth and who would make the best drinking buddy.

Jennifer is well known for being able to laugh at herself, and certainly does not take bizarre polls and accolades too seriously, but she has admitted there are downsides to having to deal with such a devoted and die-hard fan base: "I used to be very personable and make eye contact and smile at people, and now all I do is look down. When I'm at dinner and one person after another keeps interrupting to take pictures, it's like, "I can't live like this!""

CHAPTER SIX

MONEY, MONEY, MONEY

Just as her fame sky-rocketed almost overnight, Jennifer's fees shot up at a meteoric pace as soon as her film career started blossoming in 2010. She was only paid a scale rate for her role in the low-budget movie *Winter's Bone*, and because she went on to receive an Oscar nomination for that film, many people then criticised her relatively modest – considering how the movie went on to gross more than $691 million – $500,000 pay for the first *Hunger Games* instalment in 2012. But after the first film proved such a massive hit, Jennifer's army of managers and agents were able to negotiate a staggering $10 million for the sequel.

Suddenly she had unprecedented power in Hollywood, studio bosses were fighting over her, and her team were able to call all the shots. Jennifer has never wanted to talk about money or finances herself, so she is happy to leave it to the experts, who are sharply aware of her worth.

From the moment she was cast as Katniss Everdeen, Jennifer has been commanding huge pay cheques, as movie lovers, critics and industry experts alike all agree that having her name above the title of the film almost certainly guarantees success, but luckily money has never been massively important to the actress, who has garnered a reputation for being very careful not to waste her cash. Like her parents, she spends it wisely, and sensibly saves most of her earnings in a variety of lucrative investment schemes. Jennifer is rarely seen splashing her cash around on spending sprees, unlike many stars in her position. She has no interest in designer clothes or sports cars, and she prefers going home to visit her family when she has a rare few days off, rather than checking into lavish holiday resorts.

Her parents were comfortably off, but Gary and Karen worked hard for their money and never wasted it. As a result, Jennifer credits her close-knit family with keeping her feet firmly planted on the ground. 'I was raised to have value for money, to have respect for money, even though you have a lot of it,' she told *Fabulous* magazine in 2014. 'My family is not the kind of family that would ever let me turn into an asshole or anything like that, so I am fortunate to have them.'

Since she started to earn megabucks, Jennifer has become well known for her charity work and going out of her way to support a variety of worthwhile causes whenever she can. In recent years she has joined campaigns to help stamp out bullying, poverty and hunger. She also donates to a wide variety of philanthropic charities supporting the creative arts.

Then there are the causes she supports through her own charitable trust, the Jennifer Lawrence Foundation, including a fund at the Community Foundation of Louisville, DoSomething.org, Feeding America, Screen Actors Guild Foundation and the Thirst Project.

In 2012, Jennifer also starred in a promotional film for Bellewood Home for Children, a non-profit agency that has been caring for abused, neglected and homeless youths in Kentucky since 1849. In the video, she talked about the need for strong public support for the home.

And, along with her *Hunger Games* co-stars and producers, she teamed up with the World Food Program and Feeding America to raise awareness about hunger around the world. She, Josh Hutcherson and Liam Hemsworth filmed a video to encourage the public to learn more about the widespread problem, urging viewers to donate money too.

Jennifer also hosted an advance screening of *Catching Fire* for *Hunger Games* fans in her hometown of Louisville, with all the proceeds from ticket sales – which were $125 each – going to St Mary's Centre, an organisation that supports teens and adults with intellectual disabilities. The event raised more than $40,000 for the cause, which remains close to her heart. She also hosted a special screening for *Hunger Games: Mockingjay – Part 1*, also in Louisville, to benefit Boys and Girls Clubs of Kentuckiana, an out-of-school care provider which offers a safe place for youngsters to spend time.

She mentioned in an interview that it was her longstanding friendship with a boy with Down's syndrome –her childhood pal, Andy Strunk – that had inspired her to do something, and to get involved with organisations like the St Mary's Centre. Of Andy, she said 'He has the kindest heart of anyone I have ever met and is one of the funniest people I have ever been around.'

In addition to becoming an ambassador for Chideo, the charity-broadcasting network, Jennifer also agreed to contribute exclusive content for the network, as well as teaming up with fellow actor Bradley Cooper to host one lucky winner and a guest at the premiere of their most recent film, *Serena*. Fans had to donate $10 or more to their chosen causes to be in with a chance of winning the prize.

Jennifer also made a charity video saying she would be fine if she got Ebola, the highly infectious and often fatal disease which swept West Africa in 2014 – a shocking message designed to grab the viewer's attention. In the film she points out that as an American she would be lucky enough to receive treatment, and encourages her fellow countrymen to focus more on West Africans, who are far more likely to die from the dreaded virus because cures are not available to them.

The Oscar-winning actress had teamed up with her fellow stars from *The Hunger Games: Mockingjay – Part 1* once again for the two-minute online public service announcement from the Ebola Survival Fund. The video opens with a montage of clips from breathless US television news coverage of the handful of Ebola cases that have so far been reported in the United States. It then points out that none of the eight American patients treated for Ebola in US hospitals have died, while in some parts of West Africa only two out of every ten cases survive.

'A lot of them didn't make it,' said Jennifer, to which her co-star, Josh Hutcherson, replied: 'They didn't have a lot to begin with.'

'In Liberia, they had fifty doctors for 4.4 million people,' Hutcherson continued, before telling Jennifer: 'I know what would happen if you got Ebola.'

'I'd be fine,' she solemnly replied.

Liam Hemsworth, Julianne Moore and Jeffrey Wright also appeared in the hard-hitting video. But the core message came from Harvard medical professor and Partners in Health co-founder Paul Farmer, renowned for his work in developing healthcare in poor countries. Ebola patients in West Africa, he said, urgently needed IV fluids, electrolytes, food and 'many more well-trained West African medical professionals'.

Farmer added: 'With high-quality supportive care, the great majority of people in West Africa will survive Ebola.'

Around the same time, another posse of stars, including Ben Affleck, Bono, Vincent Cassel, Matt Damon and Morgan Freeman, also came together for an Ebola video sponsored by the ONE Campaign.

Apart from her charity work, Jennifer has admitted that she found her newly acquired wealth so strange she struggled to spend it at first, and rarely seemed to part with more than was strictly necessary. Until quite recently she continued to live in the same three-bedroom apartment she moved into when she first arrived in Hollywood, and although she could easily have afforded any mansion that caught her eye, it took years for her to be persuaded to make the move into a bigger place.

And unlike most A-listers, she does not have an army of staff. While there are people to manage her career decisions and work commitments, Jennifer does not see the point in hiring a team of personal assistants to do her shopping and she is very rarely found flexing her credit card in exclusive designer stores just for the sake of it – in fact she admits she loves finding a bargain just like anybody else and has been seen at holiday sales.

'I still look for bargains when I go to the market,' she admitted in an interview. 'What I am doing now is allowing someone to park my car, but for that I have to pay four bucks.'

Of course she uses valet parking when out and about in Los Angeles, since she is so busy, but she compensates by driving an economical car. While other stars rush out to spend their pay cheques on flashy Bentleys and Ferraris, Jennifer still owns the same Volkswagen that she has been driving for years, although since her Best Actress win for *Silver Linings Playbook*, she has also been spotted in a new Chevy Volt. With a $39,000 price tag, it is still about ten times cheaper than the kind of supercars she could easily afford, if she wanted to.

She has often spoken about how she cannot imagine wasting lots of money on frivolous purchases – she refuses to fork out for overpriced snacks in hotel minibars, for example. Being sensible with money is so ingrained in her lifestyle that she ended up apologetically admitting that a $500 order of Gummy Bears while hanging out with four-times Grammy Award winning rocker and *Hunger Games* co-star Lenny Kravitz had, in fact, been an accidental purchase.

However, Jennifer is loyal to those she feels she can trust, and is always very generous with her close circle of friends – as mentioned earlier, she took one of her best friends, Laura Simpson, to the Oscars in 2013. Once there they got very drunk and yelled at Brad Pitt. 'Brad Pitt and Angelina Jolie were, like, two feet away from my table,' she explained. 'And it changes you. Like, I have heart palpitations. They should be King and Queen of America. I would pay taxes to them and not even think twice about it.'

Jennifer is still best buddies with people from her high school, rather than befriending those who only want to be seen with her because she is famous now. Indeed she shrugs off people who try to get to know her because of her celebrity status. 'I just get allergic to that kind of thing,' she told *USA Today*. 'People treating you differently when you don't feel any different is really alienating. You can see the way they look at you. I can see if that was who I surrounded myself with, that's why you change. I find people who don't change. That's where I get my reality.'

She finds it difficult to hang out with some of the girls she meets on set, and has said: 'I don't trust a girl who doesn't have any girlfriends. I have really close girlfriends but they're guys like me – girls who eat and don't know anything about fashion.'

According to *E! News*, Jennifer spent just under £3,000 on a French bulldog puppy in 2014 for her old friend Laura. According to the reports, Laura uploaded a stream of cute photos of her new pet to Instagram after Jennifer found the puppy online, and then the two friends went and picked it up from the seller's home in California, with Jennifer's pooch, Pippi, along for the ride. Laura has since shared loads of photos of her new puppy, called Frankenstein, and has even created his very own Instagram account.

And perhaps she did catch the spending bug, because in November 2014 Jennifer finally found something to drop a significant chunk of her money on, when she bought a palatial home in the exclusive suburb of Beverly Crest for $8.225 million. The 5,500 square foot house, which was built in 1991, had previously belonged to singer and actress Jessica Simpson, who'd handed it over a year earlier to billionaire Sumner Redstone's girlfriend, Sydney Holland.

Jessica had hoped to sell the house for over $8 million when she put it on the market in May 2013 but ended up selling to Holland for the knockdown price of $6.4 million. Holland did not stay in the property for long, and shrewdly made a sizeable profit in just eighteen months. The French-style home boasts high ceilings, an updated kitchen, an office, five bedrooms and six bathrooms. The front of the house has a stone and floral courtyard with a koi pond, while an enviable back garden contains a sprawling lawn and a swimming pool.

Following the move to the star-studded area of Los Angeles, Jennifer discovered her neighbours included Penelope Cruz and Javier Bardem, Nicole Kidman and Keith Urban, Ashton Kutcher and Mila Kunis, as well as Cameron Diaz. While most stars tend to hire an expensive interior designer and give them free rein to buy top-of-the-range furniture, Jennifer was appalled at the idea and instead went out and bought herself a cheap sofa, vowing to take a decidedly low-key approach to furnishing her new home. She told the *Telegraph*, 'I bought one from IKEA. It was a temper tantrum but it looks great.

'It doesn't matter how much money I make, unfairness in prices really fires me up. Like shopping in LA and a T-shirt costs $150.

'I have perspective because I didn't grow up in this business. I'm not from Hollywood; I'm from Kentucky. I didn't become successful until a few years ago and I'm very aware of what the real world is and how much a couch costs.

'Humour has helped me to survive all this,' she added. 'My dad taught me always to laugh at myself. I guess I can have an intellectual conversation for five minutes, but then I want to get back to laughing.'

At the same time, Jennifer has been forced to acknowledge that the world she inhabits as an A-list movie star could not be further away from her modest Louisville upbringing, and whether she likes it or not her situation is very different now. She is without doubt extremely rich and powerful, but every time it looks as though she cannot become an even bigger star, she manages to find another way to defy expectations. And she ended 2014 as the highest-grossing actress in Hollywood. Recognising her impact on the movie industry, *Forbes* financial magazine gave her the top spot in its Most Powerful Actresses of 2014 list, as she proved that female lead actresses can also make blockbuster action movies, as well as being sex symbols. These accolades, along with her various award nominations and wins, have meant that Jennifer now ranks among the most influential stars in Hollywood.

Guinness World Records also named Jennifer the Highest-grossing Action Heroine of All Time in its 2015 edition for her role in the *Hunger Games* franchise. The latest edition of the almanac of every accomplishment, from the incredible to the odd and arcane, was also a sell-out when it hit bookstores in September 2014.

In the same year, just two of her films, *The Hunger Games: Mockingjay – Part 1* and *X-Men: Days of Future Past*, combined to make $1.4 billion at the box office. Indeed *The Hunger Games: Mockingjay – Part 1* made history when it became the top-grossing movie released in 2014.

Production company Lionsgate announced that *Mockingjay* had reached $333.2 million at the North American box office within its first few weeks of release, meaning it was the highest-earning film of 2014, beating *Guardians of the Galaxy*.

And the previous year the series experienced similar success when *Catching Fire* beat *Iron Man 3* to become 2013's biggest release. As *BuzzFeed* pointed out, it was also the second year in a row that a film with a female lead had dominated the domestic box office.

And it was also the first time in box-office history that two films in the same franchise became number one, and by then of course it was almost impossible to recall that making the first film in the series with a relative unknown in the lead had seemed like a major risk at the time.

Under the direction of Gary Ross, the very first adaptation of the popular Suzanne Collins' novel immediately smashed the box office in 2012, and not only won the top spot but did so with an starting total of $152 million.

For some idea of scale, that was $24 million more than the established superhero sequel *Iron Man 2* managed on its debut. By the time *The Hunger Games* left cinemas, the female-fronted action flick had pulled in more than $691 million worldwide, breaking box-office records and launching Jennifer to superstar status. Her share of the profits meant she would never have to work again if she chose not to.

In the winter of 2013, *The Hunger Games: Catching Fire* fared even better. It raked in $158 million on the opening weekend, $424 million in the States and $864 million worldwide. Surpassing *The Hunger Games*, the second instalment became the highest-grossing action heroine movie ever, blowing past Linda Hamilton's *Terminator 2: Judgment Day* (1991), which made $204 million in America, Angelina Jolie's *Mr. & Mrs. Smith* (2005), which took $186 million, and Sigourney Weaver's *Alien* (1979), which made $85 million.

The Hunger Games: Catching Fire also earned the title of highest domestic-grossing film of 2013, beating *Iron Man 3*. Plus, it broke into the Number 10 spot for highest domestic grossing films of all time, right behind *E.T. the Extra-Terrestrial*.

By the time the four-film franchise was halfway through, it

had already made $1.52 billion worldwide. And with excitement over *The Hunger Games: Mockingjay – Part 2* reaching fever pitch ahead of its release, Katniss's world domination looked set to continue.

Jennifer finished 2014 as the highest-grossing actor in Hollywood, with her movies taking in $1.4 billion at the worldwide box office. These figures will, of course, climb even higher when DVD sales and downloads are taken into account.

Chris Pratt finished in second place with $1.2 billion in global grosses, thanks to his starring role in Marvel's *Guardians of the Galaxy* and the Warner Bros hit comedy, *The Lego Movie*. Marvel took a risk with the outer space adventure featuring lesser known comic book characters, but Pratt as roguish hero Peter Quill resonated with audiences, and *Guardians of the Galaxy* was among the highest-grossing films ever made in the United States, with a box-office tally of $333 million.

Scarlett Johansson finished in third place with an international box-office haul of $1.18 billion, mostly from the sequel *Captain America: The Winter Soldier*, which grossed $714 million worldwide. Johansson reprised her role as Black Widow in the film starring Chris Evans as the shield-carrying superhero.

The rest of Johansson's box-office success came from her films *Lucy* and *Under The Skin*.

But despite her obvious bankability, Jennifer became embroiled in a worldwide controversy when it emerged that she had actually been paid considerably less than her male *American Hustle* co-stars.

News broke in December 2014, as a result of a damning cache of emails, which were leaked from Sony Pictures after the company's computer system was hacked, that the leading men all earned a significant amount more than the women they starred alongside. Rumours had apparently long been circulating about private dealings in the film industry, which saw the men come out on top, and the whispers were confirmed in one of those leaked emails, which revealed all of the lead actors' earnings in *American Hustle* – including the share of profits paid to Jennifer, Bradley Cooper, Christian Bale, Jeremy Renner and Amy Adams.

In emails from December 2013, executives discussed the cut of back-end profits from *American Hustle*. Director David O. Russell and actors Bradley Cooper, Christian Bale and Jeremy Renner were each paid 9 per cent of the final takings. Jennifer and her co-star Amy Adams, however, got 7 per cent for the Oscar-winning flick.

In the damning exchange of emails between co-chairman Amy Pascal, Sony Pictures president Doug Belgrad and Columbia Pictures president Andrew Gumpert, Gumpert raises the highly sensitive issue. And it was his hastily written email, which directly addressed the disparity in pay, that sparked the controversy, following its publication in *The Daily Beast*: 'Got a rush call that it's unfair the male actors get 9% in the pool and jennifer is only at 7pts. You may recall Jennifer was at 5 (amy was and is at 7) and ME wanted in 2 extra points for Jennifer to get her up to 7. If anyone needs to top jennifer up it's megan. BUT I think amy and Jennifer are tied so upping JL, ups AA.'

In the second half of the email, the Amy and AA referred to is Amy Adams, and Megan is Megan Ellison, head of co-financer Annapurna Pictures.

The same email went on to read: 'The current talent deals are: O'Russell: 9%; Cooper: 9%; Bale: 9%; Renner: 9%; Lawrence: 7%; Adams: 7%.'

To which Amy Pascal responded: 'There is truth in this.'

Jennifer was apparently originally earmarked for just 5 per cent of the film's profits, according to emails in which she is tagged by her nickname 'peanutbutt'.

According to publication *Screen Rant* and other sources, Jennifer saw a massive pay increase following her Best Actress win and the success of *X-Men*. For the *Hunger Games* sequel, *Catching Fire*, she earned $10 million, plus bonuses and escalators, placing her on the fast track to becoming one of the world's highest-paid actresses.

And she was named the second highest-paid actress of 2014, after Sandra Bullock, with estimated earnings of $34 million, thanks to her starring role in *The Hunger Games* franchise. It also emerged that *American Hustle* only got the green light to be made following the success of *The Hunger Games*.

The story became such big news because by this time Jennifer had been Hollywood's most bankable star for at least two years, and yet despite her high profile she was still subject to pay inequality – being paid 77 cents for every dollar her male co-stars made.

After breaking the story, which sparked furious news headlines around the world, a spokesman for *The Daily Beast* explained: 'The Daily Beast has combed through much of the hundreds of thousands of emails and unearthed many other shocking revelations. But the most troubling reveal concerning Lawrence is in regard to her financial compensation, with hacked emails revealing that the Hunger Games star was compensated less than her male co-stars on American Hustle.'

It is not known exactly how much the actresses were paid in the end, but these revelations were excruciating enough for the studio heads. Sony Pictures had fallen victim to a mass hack by a group referred to as the Guardians of Democracy. And many of the emails released proved incredibly embarrassing for Sony, most notably Pascal and producer Scott Rudin. Both have issued public apologies to anyone offended by any of their remarks.

And it emerged that the 25 gigabytes of data posted online by the hackers was possibly just a fraction of the terabytes stolen from Sony's computers.

Friends star Lisa Kudrow spoke out about the hacking incident, and made it clear she was not happy about the discrepancies in salaries between male and female actors. At the time she was starring in the HBO series, The Comeback, which ironically explored the modern-day entertainment industry and touched on topics such as how women are treated and judged differently from men in the notoriously sexist world of show business.

Speaking to E! News about the concepts explored in her show, and how it related to the Hollywood hacking drama, Kudrow said: 'Recently I was hearing that Jennifer Lawrence was paid the least of any of the men [actors in *American Hustle*]. Does that mean Amy Adams, too? Well, oh, that's weird? Why does that happen?

'Those women are not the draw? People are coming to see Bradley Cooper and Christian Bale? I mean, if that's a fact then that's a fact, but is that a fact? I guess is my question.'

Jennifer herself refused to comment on the scandal and when Amy Adams said she did not wish to discuss it either, she was pulled from an appearance on the *Today Show* in December 2014. She said she would not feel comfortable answering questions and as a result, producers cancelled her segment, which was meant to promote her new film, *Big Eyes*.

The Weinstein Company, the film studio responsible for *Big Eyes*, had this to say about the situation: 'We firmly stand behind Amy Adams. We've been lucky enough to have had her talents grace several of our films. We are certain her fellow actors and directors would all agree, she is nothing but the consummate professional both on and off set.

'Amy decided to speak up for herself and express her disappointment that *Today* would feel the need to ask her a question she did not feel comfortable [with], and rather than respect her opinion or continue the discussion, the reaction was to pull her appearance from the show.'

The leaked information from the Sony hack also revealed a major gap between executives' salaries. Of the seventeen Sony executives whose salary was over $1 million, just one was a woman: Sony Pictures' chair Amy Pascal herself.

The co-president of Columbia Pictures, a Sony subsidiary,

Hannah Minghella, was on track to earn $1.55 million that year, but that was actually $1 million less than male co-president Michael De Luca.

In the wake of the controversy, Oscar-winning actress Charlize Theron and her agents used the newly acquired information to renegotiate her contract for her upcoming movie *The Huntsman* – the sequel to 2012's *Snow White and the Huntsman*. Theron demanded to be paid the same amount as her co-star Chris Hemsworth. Universal Pictures reportedly agreed, offering her a new deal worth more than $10 million to avoid facing the same accusations of sexism that Sony Pictures had endured.

The revelations sparked a heated conversation through-out the industry: 'What it really reveals is how men are able to propel themselves to the top of the Hollywood food chain so quickly,' said Melissa Silverstein, founder and editor of Women and Hollywood, an organisation and website that educates, advocates and agitates for gender parity across the entertainment industry. 'Chris Hemsworth was nothing really until he got that hammer of *Thor* in his hands just a couple of years ago, and now he's able to make as much money as, or more than, an Academy Award-winning actress.'

Although the film industry has a reputation for liberal politics, she added that sexism was still rife: 'There is a narrative in Hollywood that men are more bankable.' She said she was encouraged by Charlize Theron's successful push for parity, but that her excitement was tempered by years of watching this problem go nowhere: 'Until we see some movement in these numbers, I don't think we have accomplished what we need to accomplish.'

And in an interview with *The New York Times*, actress Jennifer Aniston also spoke on the Hollywood pay disparity: 'We're very much a sexist society,' she declared. 'Women are still not paid as much as men.'

MSNBC Morning Joe co-host Mika Brzezinski chimed in too, suggesting that Jennifer should demand back pay from the producers of *American Hustle*.

'Hollywood is the perfect example of just how bad this problem is. The gap in what women are paid to their male counterparts, it's obscene.

'I think everybody whose salary was revealed, like Jennifer Lawrence, they should all speak out. They all should hold companies accountable. I would look for retroactive pay for the movie where she was paid too little.

'I'm serious. Absolutely. Because at this point, it's not going to be fixed unless you hold them to it.'

But when asked about her decision to pay Jennifer less than her male co-stars, Sony Pictures' Amy Pascal remained unrepentant, saying it was a purely commercial decision that she had to make: 'I run a business,' she stated. In February 2015 Pascal was speaking at the Women in the World event in San Francisco, where she was interviewed onstage by the legendary former editor of *Vanity Fair* and *The New Yorker*, Tina Brown.

'People should know what they're worth,' Pascal explained.

'I've paid [Jennifer Lawrence] a lot more money since then, I promise you.

'Here's the problem: I run a business. People want to work for less money; I'll pay them less money. I don't call them up and say, "Can I give you some more?"

'Because that's not what you do when you run a business. The truth is, what women have to do is not work for less money. They have to walk away.

'People shouldn't be so grateful for jobs. People should know what they're worth.'

The issue became headline news again when actress Patricia Arquette highlighted the gender pay gap in her acceptance speech after winning the Best Supporting Actress Oscar for her role in *Boyhood* in early 2015. She drew cheers from the star-studded crowd – and Meryl Streep jumped up and shouted 'Yes!' – when she said: 'To every woman who gave birth, to every taxpayer and citizen of this nation, we have fought for everybody else's equal rights.

'It's our time to have wage equality once and for all, and equal rights for women in the United States of America.'

Although she did not specifically mention the leaked Sony emails, Arquette used the attention she received on the night to speak out about the issue of gender inequality.

She went on to tell the press backstage: 'It is time for us. It is time for women. Equal means equal. And the truth is, the older women get, the less money they make. The highest percentage of children living in poverty are in female-headed households.

'It's inexcusable that we go around the world and we talk about equal rights for women in other countries and we don't have equal rights for women in America, and we don't because when they wrote the Constitution, they didn't intend it for women.'

Gender equality became the unlikely theme of the night, since Arquette was not the only actress using the high-profile ceremony to make a feminist point. When Oscar nominee Reese Witherspoon was interviewed on the red carpet, she brought up AskHerMore – an online campaign encouraging journalists to ask actresses about more than their favourite designers, or who made their dress.

'This is a movement to say we're more than just our dresses. It's hard being a woman in Hollywood,' explained Witherspoon.

But just as the issue seemed to be dying down, four months later another huge cache of hacked Sony emails was published by the whistle-blowing website *WikiLeaks*.

One message revealed the studio was forced to deal with problems that occurred as a result of Jennifer's heavy workload and back-to-back filming commitments. For months her schedule had been relentless and in January 2014 she refused to fly back to Los Angeles to shoot a glossy magazine cover for *Entertainment Weekly* with her *American Hustle* co-stars in the run-up to the Oscars. Although co-stars Bradley Cooper and Amy Adams had agreed to promote the movie with the influential US magazine, Jennifer insisted she was too tired to make the trip from where she was filming in Georgia. She also snubbed an Academy Award lunch, despite being among the nominees.

An email from Sony executive Jon Gordon said: 'Jen is definitively not coming in for the Academy luncheon. She is exhausted and the only trip she will make to LA between now and June is for the Oscars.'

Gordon's colleague Ileen Reich added: 'Jennifer Lawrence will NOT do. She won't be on another EW cover. Christian Bale will NOT do. His reps have said he doesn't do publicity once a film has opened.'

But studio boss Megan Ellison was clearly furious that Jennifer decided to turn down not only the photo shoot, but also the high-profile lunch, which would both promote the studio's films. She fired back: 'We really need to make sure Jennifer is there. I think it's a huge mistake to let her get away with not coming.'

Another studio executive, Andre Caraco, added: 'We definitely need help if we want to turn this around, including getting her to the nominees luncheon.'

The exchange revealed that the studio had spent vast sums on private planes to allow Jennifer to travel between various awards ceremonies in style, following her nomination for *American Hustle*. According to the messages, Sony spent $47,000 to charter a private jet to fly her from Atlanta to the Academy Awards, where she was contending for Best Supporting Actress.

Many of the emails discuss the various dilemmas the studio faced in trying to transport Jennifer from key award shows to film sets and back again. One message was seeking approval for a $51,000 private jet trip so Jennifer could attend the 2014 SAG Awards. Another exchange gave details of arrangements for getting the actress and her co-star Christian Bale out of stormy Atlanta for promotional commitments and then getting her back to *The Hunger Games* set to make a 6am call time.

The lengthy email from Andre Caraco read:

Information is coming in fast & furiously about the weather patterns today and how they affect private travel for Christian and Jennifer so I want to get us all on the same page.

Christian Bale: Our original plan had him doing the red carpet at the Premiere and then proceeding to the airport for a 9pm departure for Spain. Per the private aviation company, Avjet – to be 100% safe, as weather patterns rapidly change, they are suggesting that we push Christian's departure up to 6PM. The 9PM departure is still a possibility, however there is a risk involved and as you all know, there is a significant cost we are on the line for if we do not deliver him back to production in time. We need to let him know NOW so that he and his family and agents can prepare as well as alerting the jet team ASAP.

Jennifer Lawrence: Her situation is different as weather patterns in Atlanta are already compromised and we have been told that she cannot fly at the scheduled time

(8:15PM) this evening. Given that she has a 6AM call tomorrow on HUNGER GAMES, and the earliest departure time for tomorrow is 7:30AM we are being informed that the only time she can depart today in order to beat the weather is 5:00PM. Jennifer's security has connected with her and she has decided that she wants to leave at that time and the crew has been alerted as well.

Vice chairman Jeff Blake replied: 'Urgently need to know the penalty for Jennifer Lawrence not being on set of *Hunger Games* tomorrow'.

In the group email, Caraco responded that Jennifer would not travel in the bad weather. He added: 'Just to be totally clear… leaving after 5.30pm for Jennifer is not an option and her security has advised her that it is not safe and she will not do it.

'Bottom line: we are either buying her out or she leaves at 5pm.'

Eventually Jennifer agreed to attend the event, but Reich sent out a message reminding her team how to behave at the ceremony. She wrote: 'You are smiley all night no matter what. And stay in seat at end no matter what – don't get up to leave until show is over – even if it doesn't go our way. Because they could pan to our table during speech and have to look gracious no matter what.'

But the company's lavish use of private jets was a source of huge embarrassment, as it also emerged that the actor and passionate environmental campaigner Leonardo DiCaprio had flown on a private jet six times in six weeks.

DiCaprio, a high-profile advocate of environmental causes, believes the world must act now to combat the effects of global climate change and is also producing documentaries about endangered species. However, accusations of hypocrisy have dogged the Hollywood star, with detractors accusing him of not practising what he preaches.

The entire episode proved embarrassing for Sony as the studio struggled to recover from the leak. In among the scores of other revealing messages, which went public in April 2015, it was also revealed that Amy Pascal wanted to remake the film *Cleopatra* with Jennifer in the lead, but Angelina Jolie was already lined up for the role. Pascal wrote to a friend: 'I was reading old *Cleopatra* notes. I'd have to kill Angie. But the thought has crossed my mind.'

Another of Pascal's notes contained in the database explained that Jennifer and Emma Stone had indicated an early interest in starring in a remake of *Ghostbusters* with an all-female cast.

In what was widely seen as a nightmare scenario for the studio, *WikiLeaks* created a searchable database of the 30,287 Sony Pictures Entertainment documents, and 173,132 emails loaded with personal information and business dealings. In defending the decision to post the documents, *WikiLeaks* founder Julian Assange wrote on his website: 'The Sony Archives offer a rare insight into the inner workings of a large, secretive multinational corporation.

'The work publicly known from Sony is to produce

entertainment; however, The Sony Archives show that behind the scenes this is an influential corporation, with ties to the White House (there are almost 100 US government email addresses in the archive), with an ability to impact laws and policies, and with connections to the US military-industrial complex.'

Among the messages that hit the headlines, there was one about megastar singer-songwriter Bruce Springsteen, who had proved to be such a cash cow for Sony that his contract was renewed until 2027, according to an email from Sony CFO Steve Kober to Sony CEO Michael Lynton: 'Given his track record, this is not an artist that we can afford to lose. Sony Music earned approximately $72 million above the $101 million paid to Springsteen over the term.'

And in another message, actor George Clooney, who was hired to direct a film about the British tabloid phone-hacking scandal, prophetically quipped that Sony's emails might be hacked.

Other revelations included news that Tom Cruise was in talks to play Steve Jobs in a movie, Angelina Jolie was a 'minimally talented spoilt brat', and Clooney was monumentally embarrassed by *The Monuments Men* movie.

Angelina's husband Brad Pitt was also exposed for throwing a tantrum in a revealing email exchange between producers Michael De Luca and Doug Belgrad. Discussing 2014's *Fury*, Belgrad said Pitt was unhappy with some changes made to the movie: 'So Brad seems to have wigged out while watching the new cut and complained to Cynthia that he's "gutted" by the changes and threatened not to do publicity,' Belgrad wrote. 'He's also been texting with Ayer, who told me that Brad has only watched through the dinner sequence. David is hopeful that it's just a bad night or a reaction to trims or tweaks that he can easily restore.

'Cynthia is emailing Brad to try to find out more about what has triggered this and reassure him that no one will lock a cut that he doesn't feel good about. There's really nothing to do right now. Feels like we'll be dealing with whatever remaining issues there are tomorrow.'

'So weird,' De Luca responds. 'So opposite the last time we spoke to him and literally agreed with all his notes.'

The Cameron Crowe movie *Aloha*, starring Bradley Cooper, Emma Stone and Rachel McAdams, also received a lot of attention in the emails. In one exchange, Crowe and Pascal discuss the actors in the film, with the director writing: 'Our acting is better here all around. Frankly, we have great options on all the performances except Bill Murray… who pretty much is what you saw.' Pascal agrees that the movie 'belongs to Bradley'.

But Crowe then alludes to Cooper's eccentricities, saying: 'Frankly, Bradley is such an odd bird getting him right is tricky but he's fine now so lets just let him cook where he is and take care of our girl [Stone]. And her nuances — Little moves on her are huge as [you] know.'

'Getting him right was the hard part,' Pascal agrees.

Emma Stone clearly emerges as a favourite of the studio, and when Pascal emails to ask what she would like to do following the end of the *Spiderman* franchise, she makes it clear that she is tired of playing quirky, charming love interests, and replies: 'I want to play a crazy person or a bitch or something extreme really different and fun.'

In response to the creation of the searchable database, Sony accused *WikiLeaks* of contributing to the damage done by the data theft, which it condemned as 'a malicious criminal act'.

'The attackers used the dissemination of stolen information to try to harm SPE and its employees, and now *WikiLeaks* regrettably is assisting them in that effort,' Sony said in a statement.

The FBI investigated the initial hack in December 2014 and determined that it originated from North Korea in response to *The Interview*, a comedy that mocked the North Korean regime. However, some cyber security experts have said it is possible that Sony insiders could have been the culprits.

In early 2015 Amy Pascal stepped down from her high-powered post at Sony, although she later implied that she had actually been sacked. At the Women in the World conference she told journalist Tina Brown: 'All the women here are doing incredible things in the world – all I did was get fired!' She later described the experience as 'horrible but strangely freeing', although she added insult to injury by calling the celebrities she had discussed in her revealing emails as 'bottomless pits of needs'.

For Jennifer meanwhile, the whole debacle worked out rather nicely – a few months after the leak it emerged that she would finally be earning more than her male co-stars. Seen as a chance for the company to put the scandal behind them, Sony Pictures agreed that Jennifer would be paid considerably more than her co-star Chris Pratt for their upcoming movie *Passengers*. While Pratt was expected to earn a $12 million pay cheque, Jennifer's monumental deal – $20 million upfront or a 30 per cent share of the profits – was seen as ground breaking, since it still remains pretty rare for any female star to earn more than her male counterpart. And in the summer of 2015, five days after her twenty-fifth birthday, Jennifer Lawrence was named as the highest paid female actress in the world. Quite something for a happy-go-lucky girl from Kentucky.

CHAPTER SEVEN

A VERY MODERN SCANDAL

If Jennifer was left feeling uncomfortable and embarrassed about the size of her pay packet following the leak of the Sony Pictures emails, this was nothing compared to another, far more personal, hacking scandal that was to engulf her later in 2014.

She became the most famous victim of a disturbing leak of thousands of naked photos downloaded from a host of female celebrities private email and mobile phone accounts.

Jennifer did not seem hugely concerned over the salary discrepancies highlighted through the initial Sony incident – at least she did not speak out publicly. But the furore over the raunchy pictures being released to the public was considered not only a huge personal humiliation, as the images were seen by millions across the globe, but also the biggest blow to her career to date.

On 31 August 2014 a stream of incredibly intimate photos flooded onto the internet without warning, the work of anonymous hackers. As soon as Jennifer's rep confirmed the explicit nude photos splashed across the web were definitely genuine, they immediately went viral and were viewed by millions.

Jennifer was understandably mortified that her private images, apparently taken to send to a former boyfriend, were being pored over by strangers. She took the rare step of issuing a statement, which was released through her representatives and made clear how furious she was, angrily slamming the move as a 'flagrant violation of privacy'.

'The authorities have been contacted and will prosecute anyone who posts the stolen photos of Jennifer Lawrence,' her statement added.

Anonymous hackers accessed not only Jennifer's private Apple iCloud account, but also the private files of hundreds of other women in the public eye, and claimed to have scores of explicit photos of them ready to release to the public.

It quickly emerged that Jennifer was just one of many stars affected – it was rumoured as many as 423 celebrities could have been implicated in the widespread hacking operation. Although Twitter started to suspend the accounts of those who published the photos, as soon as the hack went public, an avalanche of new pictures was released, and the rapidly changing situation was becoming worse by the hour.

The photos were originally posted on the image-sharing forum *4chan*, and the anonymous hacker has since spoken out, claiming he preferred not to be known as a hacker but instead as a collector of images. But he went on to claim that he had more than sixty naked selfies of Jennifer in various compromising positions, as well as video footage of her allegedly performing a sex act.

Apple's iCloud storage system was immediately placed under heavy scrutiny as the mass hacking, which was quickly dubbed the biggest celebrity scandal in history, raised dozens of security questions about how it had been possible to access so many security protected systems without passwords.

A master list was printed with names of many of the other alleged victims who had fallen prey to the hackers, which was said to have included both British and American actors, models, reality stars and musicians including Rihanna, Michelle Keegan, Cara Delevingne, Cat Deeley, Kelly Brook, *Glee* star Lea Michele, Aubrey Plaza, Candice Swanepoel, Hilary Duff, Kaley Cuoco, Kim Kardashian, Selena Gomez, Vanessa Hudgens, Kate Bosworth, Victoria Justice, Emily Browning, Jenny McCarthy and Hayden Panettierre – all apparently in similar compromising positions.

Horrified Twitter users quickly rallied round to support Jennifer after the explicit photos of her were shared online, and many people refused to look at them as a matter of principle.

One user declared: 'I'd be quite proud if I looked like #JenniferLawrence'.

'So the person who leaked Jennifer Lawrence's nudes has lists and lists of names he has and I feel so sorry for them,' added another fan.

But some users could not hide their glee and excitement about having free access to what could be considered pornographic images, as the photos took over their Twitter feed.

'Today is a good day,' wrote one fan.

'The best way to start the week,' added another.

Until that fateful day *4chan* was just a little-known website where users could anonymously post photos and videos, as well as comment on others' posts. Users did not need to register an account before participating, so it was entirely unregulated.

The site was split into various boards, each with its own specific content from video games and music to photography and snaps people wanted to share of their favourite celebrities. Many fans urged police to find those responsible for setting up and maintaining the site, while singer Ariana Grande and actress/singer Victoria Justice came forward, saying the photos of them were fake.

Model Kate Upton confirmed there were genuine photos of her that had been leaked, and her lawyer issued a statement on her behalf, saying: 'This is obviously an outrageous violation of our client Kate Upton's privacy. We intend to pursue anyone disseminating or duplicating these illegally obtained images to the fullest extent possible.'

Upton later told the *Evening Standard*: 'It was very difficult. It's an invasion of my privacy and it's not OK. It's illegal. People don't have a right to look at those photos or to judge them.' She added that she had fantasised about leaving social media sites including Twitter and Instagram, but had been unable to do so because they were important for professional purposes.

Above left: A young Jennifer at the 2008 6th Annual Teen Vogue Hollywood Party in LA.   © *Michael Buckner/Getty Images*

Above right: The 'over-the-shoulder' pose before the screening of *The Burning Plain* in 2008.   © *Alberto Pizzoli/AFP/Getty Images*

Below: Another screening, this time of *Winter's Bone* in 2010.

© *Alexandra Wyman/WireImage*

Above: There's no getting away! Jennifer locks co-star Josh Hutcherson in a headlock as they attend *The Hunger Games: Catching Fire* premiere in Rome, 2013.

© Vittorio Zunino Celotto/Getty Images

Below left: Jennifer with her fellow *Hunger Games* stars, Liam Hemsworth, Josh Hutcherson and Elizabeth Banks at the London O2 Arena in 2012.

© Jon Furniss/WireImage

Below right: The Girl on Fire times two, at another 2013 premiere of *The Hunger Games: Catching Fire* in Madrid.

© Carlos Alvarez/Getty Images

Above: The curse of the Academy Awards: Jennifer falls over at the Oscars for the second year running, as she receives her award for Best Actress for her role in *Silver Linings Playbook* in 2013.

Below: Well worth falling over for, Jennifer shows off her Academy Award.

Above: It's not called the Late Show for nothing. Jen tucks herself in as she chats to David Letterman in 2013.   © *Jeffrey R. Staab/CBS via Getty Images*

Below: Smiles all round; speaking onstage with her fellow *Hunger Games* star Elizabeth Banks at ELLE's 21st Annual Women in Hollywood Celebration in 2014.   © *Michael Buckner/Getty Images*

Ready for the after party of the 2014 World Premiere of *The Hunger Games: Mockingjay – Part 2* in London.
© David M. Benett/WireImage

Above: The *American Hustle* stars smiling for the cameras, ready to win their Golden Globe awards in Beverly Hills, California, 2014.

© *George Pimentel/WireImage*

Below left: As glam as ever, Jennifer sits in the front row beside Dior CEO Sidney Toledano and fashion icon Emma Watson, during the 2014 Paris Fashion Week.

© *Rindoff/Dufour/French Select/Getty Images*

Below right: 'Am I over-dressed?' Pippi rocks the bowtie, alongside a more casual Jen as she's spotted in LA in June 2015.

© *GVK/Bauer-Griffin/GC Images*

Above: Exchanging cheesy grins with Bradley Cooper at the after party of the March 2015 *Serena* screening in New York City.   © *Dimitrios Kambouris/WireImage*

Below: Still smiling with Josh and Liam on *The Hunger Games: Mockingjay – Part 2* panel at the 2015 Comic-Con International Santiago Convention.

© *Albert L. Ortega/Getty Images*

Jennifer Lawrence,
the Girl on Fire.

Equally horrified, Jennifer refused to make any apologies about keeping naked pictures of herself on her computer, and hit back at the hackers who stole the provocative shots during an emotional interview for a cover feature in *Vanity Fair* magazine's November 2014 edition. Speaking about the photo-theft incident for the first time, Jennifer said: 'It is not a scandal. It is a sex crime. It is a sexual violation. It's disgusting. The law needs to be changed, and we need to change.'

She went on to say that the law should be rewritten so those responsible for any violation of privacy could be prosecuted like all other sex offenders, including rapists and paedophiles, adding anyone who had viewed the explicit pictures should 'cower with shame'.

But her fury turned to sadness as she explained how she had taken the nude selfies for her boyfriend at the time, and although she did not name him in the interview, it was believed to be actor Nicholas Hoult as they spent much of their relationship apart due to conflicting filming schedules.

The couple met while co-starring in 2011's *X-Men: First Class*, and in one interview Jennifer had said that they liked having a long-distance relationship as it meant they could keep their independence.

'I was in a loving, healthy, great relationship for four years,' she told *Vanity Fair* in November 2014. 'It was long distance, and either your boyfriend is going to look at porn or he's going to look at you.'

She also admitted that she had been incredibly concerned about the effect the leak would have on her work opportunities at a point when she had just become a huge star: 'I was just so afraid. I didn't know how this would affect my career.

'Just because I'm a public figure, just because I'm an actress, does not mean that I asked for this,' she said. 'It's so beyond me. I just can't imagine being that detached from humanity. It does not mean that it comes with the territory.

'It's my body, and it should be my choice, and the fact that it is not my choice is absolutely disgusting. I can't believe that we even live in that kind of world.'

When the photos were first leaked over the internet, Jennifer recalled that she had sat down and tried to compose a statement, but the right words were hard to find. 'Every single thing that I tried to write made me cry or get angry. I started to write an apology, but I don't have anything to say I'm sorry for,' she told *Vanity Fair*.

'Just the fact that somebody can be sexually exploited and violated, and the first thought that crosses somebody's mind is to make a profit from it. It's so beyond me.

'Even people who I know and love say, "Oh, yeah, I looked at the pictures." I don't want to get mad, but at the same time I'm thinking, "I didn't tell you that you could look at my naked body".'

Another major consequence was that she had to break the news to her father that naked images of her were available to be viewed by millions of people online. Fortunately, Gary took the news far better than she expected.

Jennifer explained: 'I don't care how much money I get for *The Hunger Games*, I promise you, anybody given the choice of that kind of money or having to make a phone call to tell your Dad that something like that has happened, it's not worth it.'

Actress Jennifer Garner also suggested that those who looked at the photos were guilty of more than just casual curiosity. Speaking to *Loaded* magazine in the aftermath of the leak, she said: 'It's an invasion. It's violent. It's a violent abuse of women. It just makes me want to hurt somebody.'

The day after the leak became worldwide news, the anonymous uploader behind the scandal spoke out for the first time, saying he was disappointed by how little money he had made from the controversial move.

Posting on *4chan*, using the same IM (Instant Messaging) as the person who posted the snaps of Jennifer, he wrote: 'I didn't take the money and run. S★★8 got weird once I started posting samples.

'People wanted shit for free. Sure, I got $120 with my bitcoin [a form of digital currency] address, but when you consider how much time was put into acquiring this stuff (I'm not the hacker, just a collector), and the money (I paid a lot via bitcoin as well to get certain sets when this stuff was being privately traded Friday/Saturday) I really didn't get close to what I was hoping.'

He went on to claim to have video footage of Jennifer and said that his organisation would be accepting PayPal donations in exchange for viewing the brief film.

In the post he added: 'I know no one will believe me, but I have a short Lawrence video. Is way too short, a little over 2 minutes and you only get to see her boobs. Anyways, if somebody wants it let me know how i can upload it anonymously (i don't want the FBI over me, and you don't wanna know how I got this video.)'

The alleged hackers claimed to have stolen the snaps from Apple's iCloud Photostream service, which automatically shares iPhone photos with all of the user's other computer devices and tablets, and stores them online, calling into question how secure the password-protected system really was.

It was thought that the hacker could have gained access simply by guessing the stars' passwords, or resetting their accounts by gaining access to their email addresses and answering the few relevant security questions required.

Bryan Hamade, the man behind the hugely popular online forum *Reddit* – which was thought to be behind a previous Apple iCloud hack – was forced to deny that he was responsible for the nude photo leak: 'I am not the original leaker. The real guy is on *4chan* posting intermittently,' Hamade told the *Daily Mail*.

At first *Reddit* had been among the sites to spread the intimate photos of many stars, including Jennifer and even Olympic gold-winning gymnast McKayla Maroney, who was pictured underage. Although *Reddit* pulled the posts after heavy pressure from the celebrities and their lawyers, the site kept plenty of other boards alive, which featured stolen compromising images of ordinary people – mostly women and many of them ex-girlfriends of bitter subscribers to the site. The site's administrators were roundly criticised for having one rule for celebrities, another for normal people.

But after a few months the company bowed to pressure and decided to be a little more proactive, starting to crack down on unauthorised photos whether or not those pictured were famous. *Reddit* vowed to crack down on the unauthorised posting of private nude photos. The promise was made in a larger blog post about planned administrative changes to the site. Under the proposed new policy, *Reddit* would scrub itself clean of a racy and compromising sexy picture if someone in the snap complained that the image was uploaded without their permission. 'Last year, we missed a chance to be a leader in social media when it comes to protecting your privacy – something we've cared deeply about since *Reddit*'s inception,' the blog read. 'At our recent all hands company meeting, this was something that we all, as a company, decided we needed to address.

'No matter who you are, if a photograph, video, or digital image of you in a state of nudity, sexual excitement, or engaged in any act of sexual conduct is posted or linked to on *Reddit* without your permission, it is prohibited on *Reddit*.'

The post was clearly referring to the mega-leak of nude photos stolen from Apple iCloud accounts, which later became known as 'The Fappening', a popular way to describe the hack.

Of course there were those who felt little sympathy for the stars who were embarrassed by the leaks, and some even suggested they should never have taken such explicit pictures in the first place.

In a bid to promote password security, Strathclyde University produced a poster, saying: 'Bet Jennifer Lawrence wishes she'd used a StR0nG_Pas5w0Rd%.' The image attracted widespread criticism on social media, with the Glasgow-based university being accused of 'victim blaming'. An image of the poster was tweeted by one student, who said: 'Pretty shocking victim blaming here. Will you take it down?'

It was soon withdrawn, and the university said the poster should never have been made. Strathclyde University tweeted: 'The posters are being removed now. They should not have produced and we are looking into how this happened.'

A spokesman for the university later said: 'The posters are in bad taste and have now been removed from campus. The sentiment expressed is not consistent with the values of this university.'

Within hours of the high-profile leaks becoming public knowledge, the very first steps were being taken to consider how the law might address such theft, and Jennifer found herself at the centre of key political debates. The Congressional Internet Caucus Advisory Committee held a meeting to discuss the topic, entitled 'Jennifer Lawrence's Hacked Photos: A "Sex Crime?" The Legal Underpinnings of Digitally Exposed Private Images and What Congress Needs to Know'.

Among the influential speakers were Mary Anne Franks, associate professor of law at the University of Miami School of Law, and Emma Llansó, director of the Free Expression Project at the Center for Democracy & Technology.

The advisory committee asked the very important question:

'What kind of legal recourse does Jennifer Lawrence – or an everyday American citizen like you – have against hackers and websites that peddle such photos?'

The aim was to analyse exactly what contemporary expectations of privacy are in a realm of digital photography, from revenge porn to so-called 'up skirt' pictures taken by pushy paparazzi photographers in broad daylight. The committee discussed the suggestion that almost daily there are incidents of some kind involving stolen photos of women – the same day as it emerged that a police officer in California had stolen private photos from the phone belonging to a woman he had arrested, a practice he had allegedly described as 'a game'.

However, the advisory committee itself is not a government institution. Rather, it is a private sector organisation, where representatives of all interested stakeholders – from corporations to private interest groups – meet. The purpose is to discuss how to ensure that members of the Congressional Internet Caucus, and Congress members in general, understand issues about which they may have to have an opinion at some stage in their working lives. The committee used the Twitter hashtag #exposedphotos to attract global attention to its event.

But as they discussed at length, the problem of all legislation when it comes to the web is that technology always moves faster than the law – legislate against one type of activity and someone will find another way to achieve his ends.

Tech experts said at the time that weak passwords had given hackers the chance to access private pictures, thanks to a software glitch, and Apple agreed to conduct an investigation into the scandal after dozens of A-listers' passwords were stolen by a particularly sophisticated piece of hacking software.

Soon after the leak, a key piece of computer code that repeatedly guessed passwords was found online. The script was posted to software site *GitHub*, but a message quickly appeared saying that Apple had issued a 'patch' or fixes to eliminate the bug. According to the post, the script used the top 500 most common passwords approved by Apple in order to try and gain access to user accounts. If successful, it would give the hacker full access to the iCloud accounts, and therefore photos.

Owen Williams from technology site *The Next Web*, who discovered the bug, said: 'The Python script found on *GitHub* appears to have allowed a malicious user to repeatedly guess passwords on Apple's "Find my iPhone" service without alerting the user or locking out the attacker.

'Given enough patience and the apparent hole being open long enough, the attacker could use password dictionaries to guess common passwords rapidly. Many users use simple passwords that are the same across services so it's entirely possible to guess passwords using a tool like this.

'If the attacker was successful and gets a match by guessing passwords against Find my iPhone, they would be able to, in theory, use this to log into iCloud and sync the iCloud Photo Stream with another Mac or iPhone in a few minutes, again, without the attacked user's knowledge.

'We can't be sure that this is related to the leaked photos, but the timing suggests a possible correlation.'

Apple did not make any comment on the incident, but

experts pointed to the weakness of many internet users' passwords and basic security knowledge as being the cause for the widespread hack of iCloud – Apple's own wireless storage facility that can be used to access files remotely.

Other similar services include Dropbox and Google Drive, which enable users to keep more of their files close at hand without taking up huge amounts of memory on their devices.

Rob Cotton, CEO at web security experts NCC Group, said: 'Cyber security is not just a technology problem, humans are very much key to its success. In our day-to-day work we see too many cases of employees divulging sensitive information without first verifying the legitimacy of the request.

'People often point the finger at technology when they've been the victim of a cyber attack, but poor password choices or naivety in the face of a seemingly innocent email is regularly to blame.'

He added that human error often played a part too.

Stefano Ortolani, security researcher at online experts Kaspersky Lab, added: 'In order to make your private data more secure, you should cherry-pick the data you store in the cloud and know and control when the data is set to automatically leave your device.

'For instance, in iCloud there is a feature called My Photo Stream which uploads new photos to the cloud as soon as the device is connected to Wi-Fi; this is to keep photos synchronised across all your devices. Disabling this option might be a good starting point to be a bit more in control.'

While the security of the cloud will now come under

increased scrutiny, Ortolani pointed out that some element of risk has always existed.

He said: 'The security of a cloud service depends on its provider.

'However, it's important to consider that as soon as you hand over any data including photos to a third-party service, you need to be aware that you automatically lose some control of it. This is also the case for when you upload something online.'

Within weeks of the scandal, a man claiming to be Jennifer's ex-boyfriend admitted that he was a computer hacker. Brad Jackson, who alleged that he dated Jennifer when they were pre-teens growing up in Louisville, made the revelation in conversation with the *Sun on Sunday* about the breach of privacy she suffered: 'She's the type of person who would have done a nude scene but would have wanted to make the decision on her own,' he said.

'The fact a hacker did it [leaked the pictures] was pretty shitty – but that's the kind of field I'm in.'

The IT graduate went on to claim that he had seen the computer screen of a man claiming to have been the person who accessed Lawrence's private photographs through her computer without her permission. He went on to claim that he is not a 'black hat' hacker, like those who work for *4chan*, but would be lured into hacking by the profit he could make from it.

'I'm so tempted to go into the illegal part and make more money,' he told the newspaper.

Jennifer has since said that she cannot let her happiness rest on those responsible being brought to justice, because most likely they will never be caught, adding she just has to find her own peace.

As already discussed, it was widely believed that Jennifer had taken the private photos to send to her then boyfriend Nicholas Hoult, and the British actor was asked about the leak while chatting with *Good Day New York* about his upcoming film, *Young Ones*.

'It's shocking that things like that happen in the world,' he said. 'It's a shame.'

The scandal became rich fodder for comedians who suggested it could have been avoided simply by not taking such explicit photos in the first place. Ricky Gervais was forced to issue a public apology after he wrote on Twitter: 'Celebrities, make it harder for hackers to get nude pics of you from the computer by not putting nude pics of yourself on your computer.'

And the satirical cartoon *South Park* also poked fun at Jennifer's situation, but Jennifer's *Hunger Games* co-star Josh Hutcherson was among those who rushed to her defence, saying: 'I just think all that stuff is so ridiculous. We're people, too, man, we just want to live. We want to be normal people, it's not fair.

'I think everyone has their own way of getting through it. It's something you obviously don't want to happen to you and it's really unfortunate that it happens. I hate the way the world sort of views those sorts of issues.'

Josh said he and Jennifer often talked about how experiencing sudden fame on a huge scale had changed every aspect of their lives: 'Like Jen and I always say, people say, "Well you chose to be an actor, you are going to have to deal with this kind of thing." Well, no. I started when I was nine years old. She started when she was, like, twelve.

'We didn't choose to have public scandal. So because this is what I am good at and this is my career means I also have to suffer on this other side?'

Actress Sigourney Weaver also praised the dignified way in which Jennifer had dealt with the humiliation surrounding the leak, and expressed her admiration for how she had been forced to live her life under constant scrutiny: 'There is no escape now,' said the *Alien* star. 'It's something actors need to figure out how to combat, as it doesn't serve anyone to have privacy invaded to such an extent.

'Jennifer is brilliant. Leave her alone. But I'm a grandmother practically,' Sigourney told *The Sunday Times* newspaper.

Natalie Dormer, the actress who starred alongside Jennifer in the final two *Hunger Games* movies, also came out in support of her co-star: 'What Jen went through recently was just horrific,' she told *Nylon* magazine. 'And I don't think there's any level of fame that can justify that kind of invasion into privacy, not to mention laws being broken. I mean, people just need to get a grip if they think that's even halfway acceptable.'

Spider-Man star Andrew Garfield also spoke out on Jennifer's behalf, slamming the hackers who stole nude photos of women and posted them online as misogynistic. The actor told *The Daily Beast*: 'It's disgusting. "I have a right to your naked body or images that you've sent to your husband, or lover". It's disgusting. It's violent, and it's misogynistic, and it's revolting, and it's another example of what this distance [through the internet] has enabled us to do – it's enabled us to be disassociated from each other.

'There's enough awful shit coming from it that hopefully we'll get to the point of, "OK, wait a second." What's scary is that we haven't reached that point yet, and there hasn't been a referendum put on it.'

Meanwhile, Jennifer was forced to condemn the actions of Perez Hilton, the celebrity blogger who initially published the images uncensored, before deleting them from his widely read site and issuing a personal apology to Jennifer.

'[Perez] took it down because people got pissed, and that's the only reason why,' she said. 'And then I had to watch his apology. And what he basically said was, "I just didn't think about it." "I just didn't think about it" is not an excuse. That is the exact issue itself.'

Perez later admitted that he had 'made a mistake' in publishing the actress's intimate images on his website, and claimed that he did not wish to harm others with his work. When asked what prompted this unexpected change of heart, he said: 'I look at mistakes as an opportunity to learn. I made a mistake and instead of not doing anything I decided not to post any photos of anybody like that going forward, which I haven't.'

Speaking about the apology he gave Jennifer, Perez added:

'I've been trying to do better and be better for four years now. I'm not perfect, I'm not trying to be, but it's a constant journey and a process.'

In the meantime, Jennifer was devastated yet further when it emerged that there were plans for some of the stolen nude celebrity photos to be publicly displayed in an exhibit at an American art gallery. A then anonymous artist, known only as XVALA, real name Jeff Hamilton, intended to use the images as part of their show titled 'No Delete' in the Cory Allen Art Gallery in St. Petersburg, Florida.

When asked about the controversial plans, actor Andrew Garfield responded furiously: 'The internet is the new Wild West. There's a guy now taking these pictures and putting them up in an art gallery. What right does he have to do that? It's absolutely revolting.'

But following public backlash, and pressure from a petition, the artist changed his mind. XVALA decided not to showcase leaked images of the celebs in life-size, unaltered form; instead the exhibit would feature the artist's self-shot, life-size nude images: 'It wasn't just about being "hacked" images anymore, but now presented in the media as stolen property,' XVALA said in a statement to *E! News*. 'People were identifying with Jennifer Lawrence's and Kate Upton's victimisation, much more than I had anticipated, which is powerfully persuasive.'

Gallery owner Cory Allen added: 'It was inspiring to see people take action through a petition, signing their name and not just commenting on a thread.'

Just a few days earlier, both Allen and XVALA said they

were proceeding with the art show despite public outrage, claiming the images were 'art'. But then they claimed that once their goal of raising public awareness had been accomplished, they were willing to cancel the show and to move on: 'This concept was always about self-examination in our current culture,' XVALA said. 'Why we feel the need to know and cross the lines of other individuals' privacy.'

Jennifer was delighted when Google agreed to pull links to the nude photos from their search engine. Google came under pressure from many lawyers representing various celebrities whose private photos were published by hackers. But according to the *Guardian* newspaper, the decision was only made in a bid to combat the numerous lawsuits filed against the technology giant. 'Google has come under pressure from lawyers representing various celebrities whose private photos were published by hackers,' the newspaper claimed. 'The top entertainment lawyer Martin Singer has written to Google demanding that the company pay for its "blatantly unethical behaviour", threatening to sue the search giant for $100 million.'

Singer's Los Angeles-based firm Lavely & Singer P.C. represents more than a dozen of the women affected, as well as actors including John Travolta and Charlie Sheen. Lavely & Singer wrote to various website operators and Internet Service Providers (ISPs) demanding that the images be taken down under the Digital Millennium Copyright Act (DMCA).

Repeating its statement from early October 2014, Google said: 'We've removed tens of thousands of pictures – within hours of the requests being made – and we have closed hundreds of accounts. The internet is used for many good things. Stealing people's private photos is not one of them.'

Google removed two links to a site hosting stolen nude photos of Jennifer, following demands from her lawyers. The takedown requests were filed under the DMCA, with her lawyers stating that the stolen photos impinged on Lawrence's copyright. The DMCA, which governs the use of copyrighted material and is usually used in reference to pirated TV shows, films and music, requires sites to 'expeditiously' remove unlawful images from their servers.

The site removed from Google's search results has since changed its domain, which has caused the site to be re-indexed by Google and reappear in search results under a different website address. The takedown notice did not list the new domain, requiring another request to be filed to remove it from the search results.

The site hosting the photos targeted by Jennifer's lawyer claimed that it would take down the stolen photos, if requested.

The whole hacking debacle made Jennifer more wary than ever of using the internet, indeed she shies away from any social-networking sites, unlike most celebrities of her generation: 'I will never get Twitter,' she explained in an interview with Radio1 DJ Nick Grimshaw: 'I'm not very good on phone or technology. I cannot really keep up with emails, so the idea of Twitter is so unthinkable to me.

'I don't really understand what it is. It's like this weird enigma that people talk about. It's fine, I respect that, but no,

I'll never get a Twitter. If you ever see a Facebook, Instagram or Twitter that says it's me, it most certainly is not.

'I really, like, laser focused on that. It's because the internet has scorned me so much that I feel like it's that girl in high school that I'm like, "Oh, you want to talk about her? Yeah, I'll do that! Take my hoops off, I'm ready to go."

'All that doesn't interest me for a second. I'm always hundreds of emails behind. I have 112 unread emails,' she added, holding up her phone. 'I don't want anyone to talk to me, ever.'

Jennifer was far from alone in her horror at the leak. Former *Harry Potter* star Emma Watson said in March 2015 that she too was left 'raging' after a hoax website threatened to release nude photos of her online. The film star and UN Ambassador for Women said a website targeted her after she spoke up for women's rights.

She said: 'After I gave my speech [at the UN] there was a website threatening to release naked pictures of me. I knew it was a hoax, I knew the pictures didn't exist, but I think a lot of people that were close to me knew gender equality was an issue but didn't think it was that urgent, that it was a thing of the past.

'And then when they saw that the minute I stood up talking about women's rights I was immediately threatened, I think they were really shocked, my brother was particularly upset.

'This is a real thing that's happening now, women are receiving threats. I was raging, it made me so angry. I was like, this is why I have to be doing this. If anything, if they were trying to put me off it, it did the opposite.'

In September 2014, a web page entitled 'Emma You Are Next', featuring an image of the actress next to a countdown clock, appeared to have been created by a user of *4chan*, on which the nude photos of Jennifer Lawrence had been posted.

Months later it emerged that 'The Fappening' had significantly changed the way in which British people send raunchy text messages, but it had not altered the number of them doing it, according to research released in March 2015. Three quarters of British men and women apparently changed their sexting habits after the online scandal, which saw almost 100 celebrities' private nude photographs hacked, with many taking extra security precautions.

Globally, during 2014, the number of men 'sexting' increased by 2.5 per cent, while there was a 9 per cent increase in the number of women sexting. Of these women, 72 per cent claimed they were sending and storing their messages more securely. In comparison, 68 per cent of men said they were changing their habits. The Fappening mainly targeted young female celebrities and prompted a huge discussion over online privacy and protection.

The survey, titled 'Apps and Appetites', also found that one in four – 26 per cent of men and 22 per cent of women – had not changed their habits at all, despite the publicity the significant data breaches received.

Almost 75,000 people around the world responded to the survey by *AshleyMadison.com*, an extramarital affairs website, examining how technology affected trends in sexual behaviour.

'Technology has revolutionised so many facets of life, including infidelity, that it is no surprise to see habits changing in response to these major violations of individuals' privacy,' said spokesman Christoph Kraemer.

But the research also found that two thirds of men and women, despite the online scandal, still sexted with the same frequency, with an overall increase in 2014.

Globally, more women (79.6 per cent) than men (87.2 per cent) say they sext – but in the UK almost 10 per cent fewer women admit to the practice, with a similar proportion of British men sexting. Almost half of those surveyed also confessed to sexting on the job, with 46 per cent of men (a 2.5 per cent increase) and 40 per cent of women (7.5 per cent increase) admitting to sending sexts during working hours.

For months the police continued to hunt for those responsible for embarrassing so many unwitting celebrities. In June 2015, FBI agents raided the Chicago home of Emilio Herrera whose IP address was allegedly used to hack more than 500 iCloud accounts, including Jennifer's.

Special agent Josh Sedowsky wrote in official FBI documents, 'Based on victim account records obtained by Apple, one or more computers at Herrera's house accessed or attempted to access without authorisation multiple celebrities' email and iCloud accounts over the course of several months.' As well as Jennifer, the documents listed other victims including actresses Christina Hendricks, Olivia Wilde and Amber Heard.

But at the time of writing, Herrera had not been charged with any crimes, and Jennifer had refused to comment on the news. She had already made her feelings perfectly clear on the subject with her customary directness and dignity.

CHAPTER EIGHT

A POP STAR
IN THE MAKING

One thing that Jennifer and Coldplay frontman Chris Martin have in common is a shared love of music, and it can be no coincidence that their romance started to blossom just as she recorded her first single – 'The Hanging Tree', a haunting folk song taken from the soundtrack of *The Hunger Games: Mockingjay – Part 1*.

For many actors, the moment that the last instalment of a franchise hits the cinemas can be a difficult stage in their career, as they find themselves wondering if they can continue their early success.

When the stars of *Harry Potter*, including Daniel Radcliffe and Emma Watson, or *Twilight*'s Kristen Stewart and Robert Pattinson reached the end of the blockbuster film series that made them stars, they had to prove to Hollywood that they were more than just the lucky beneficiaries of can't-miss roles, and battle to be taken seriously as adults, and not to be typecast in the same kind of roles.

Jennifer was not to be faced with that problem, however, thanks to strong performances in a variety of movies like *X-Men*, *American Hustle* and *Silver Linings Playbook*, as well as revealing hidden musical talents. On top of trying her hand at action, comedy and drama, she was also smart enough to branch out, setting her sights on the music world, after her debut release triumphed in the music charts around the world.

'The Hanging Tree' landed at Number 12 on America's Billboard Hot 100, raking in more than 200,000 downloads within its first few days. It went on to sell over 1.1 million copies, and Jennifer also scored a Top 20 hit in the UK charts.

In the film, her character Katniss Everdeen performed the song she had learnt from her father. Her rendition the haunting, bluesy piece, which became a rallying cry for rebellion in the Districts, was seen as one of the more moving sequences.

The song, which also appears on the film's official soundtrack, was written by The Lumineers' Jeremiah Fraites and Wesley Schultz, with lyrics by *Hunger Games* author Suzanne Collins.

Schultz told *Billboard* that *Mockingjay* director Francis Lawrence explained to him that the song had 'to be something that can be hummed or sung by one person [or] by a thousand people' and that it couldn't be 'overly complicated'.

He added: 'It's supposed to almost feel like a nursery rhyme, innocent, even though it has a really dark undertone to it.'

Schultz and Fraites submitted several melodies in September

2013, and Schultz recalled producers eventually choosing one and telling them: 'This one seems promising, let's do this.'

But the pair were still not sure their tune would be used in such a big movie, and they assumed there were other, far more famous songwriters in the running: 'Probably a lot of people were trying to write a melody. I just don't think we really had our hopes up.'

Despite their lack of confidence the song's use in the film clearly moved audiences, who downloaded it in their droves.

'The first time that I heard it was going to be [officially in the film] was through Francis Lawrence,' Schultz added. 'He texted us and said, "It worked out great in the movie. We just shot the scene. Jen was really nervous but it went great."'

Jennifer suddenly found herself climbing high in the charts, just behind the likes of Taylor Swift, who was Number 1 for a third week running with her song, 'Blank Space', and Maroon 5, who took the fifth spot for 'Animals'.

The song even beat the film's official pop single, Lorde's 'Yellow Flicker Beat'. And according to *Billboard*, Jennifer was the thirteenth Oscar winner to grab a spot on the list, sharing the honour with superstars Bing Crosby, Julie Andrews, Cher, Jamie Foxx, Meryl Streep and Jennifer Hudson.

'The Hanging Tree' also made it on to the UK music charts, and reached Number 8 on the midweek iTunes countdown, even though it had not yet been officially released as a single at that point.

Jennifer was stunned when she heard that she had beaten Meghan Trainor's 'Lips Are Moving', the Jessie J/

Ariana Grande/Nicki Minaj collaboration, 'Bang Bang', and Beyoncé's '7/11'. The chart placing proved a massive shock for the actress, who had broken down in tears before filming her singing scene because she was dreading it so much.

Francis Lawrence explained to *Radio Times* magazine: 'She was horrified to sing. She cried a little bit in the morning before [the scene]. She'd probably tell you it was her least favourite day on set.

'She'll probably never really understand it because she's so sensitive about the singing, but she did it and she did it all day, and she hated me for making her do it all day, but she did and it's great.'

Jennifer was so nervous before her performance that she refused to even show off her voice in rehearsals. The director continued: 'We had a vocal coach, who sort of shifted the key for Jen's voice. Then she started working with Jen once or twice. Jen didn't really want to do too much of the training. I was worried, I really thought we were going to have to do a bunch of pitch shifting, but she sounded great.

'What you hear in the movie is what she did on the day in the quarry.'

The movie, the third instalment of the hit fantasy series, shot to the top of the US box office as soon as it was released in November 2014, with early takings of over $122 million, and it fared equally well in the UK, raking in over £12 million within its first few days on the big screen.

But apparently Jennifer had been scarred by a childhood experience in which her mother – trying to be supportive –

had encouraged her to sing in front of her entire school. Jennifer later claimed the performance was a total embarrassment. She had only been eight years old when she belted out 'Have a Holly, Jolly Christmas', and the actress admitted that even her father laughed for days about her rendition of the catchy Christmas song.

So when she learned that her character Katniss would have to perform a song in the film, Jennifer apparently broke down in tears at the memory of the last time she had sung in front of an audience. It seemed she refused to even listen to the song, but she has recounted the 'traumatic' story of eventually having to sing it in front of the rest of the cast and crew.

In a television interview with David Letterman she explained: 'I don't like singing in front of people. It's my biggest fear. I cried on set. I sang "The Hanging Tree", which is where I felt like going.'

Time and again she has admitted in interviews that singing on the film was the most terrifying thing she has ever done. 'I can't stand singing. The idea of singing in front of people is my biggest fear in the entire world. I cried the day that I did that,' she told *HitFix*. 'I was shaking. I was like, "I want my mom." I've never listened to it. When that scene comes on, I plug my ears.

'I cried on set that day and apparently I'm crying all the time,' she added. 'I'm like, scarred from my childhood because I have a Southern mother who would just tell me that I was amazing at everything, that I could do everything. But, I can't.'

Jennifer also told *The New York Times* an anecdote about

how she felt she has always had a 'tone-deaf Amy Winehouse' voice, adding: 'I think I sound like a hermit, a deep, chain-smoking hermit.'

And when asked about it on *Saturday Night Live* she said that her singing sounded like 'a deer that has been caught in a fence'.

But Francis Lawrence defended his leading lady's talents, adding: 'There are very few times when Jen gets nervous about stuff she has to do on set, and the singing was that kind of a thing. I knew she didn't love the idea of singing, but I didn't realise how nervous she was until when we started the first take, and she was in tears.

'Not totally broken down, but she was unhappy. I didn't have to talk her into it, she was going to do it, she knew it was her job, but she just wasn't happy about it. "Oh man, I've got to actually sing! In front of 150 people!"

'She would have much rather we used somebody else's voice. I think she said she wanted Lorde to do it! But see, the thing on top of all of it is, it shouldn't sound like a professional. It should sound like a real girl singing. So she did it. She did it all day.

'And she has a really cool sound to her voice. There's kind of a raspy texture to it. So it was not terrible in the slightest.'

Jennifer may have been modest about her success but everyone heard the song, whether they liked it or not. During an interview with Ryan Seacrest on *E!*'s *Live From the Red Carpet* ahead of the 2015 Oscars, Josh Hutcherson, who was presenting at the ceremony, was asked whether or not he had

'The Hanging Tree' on his phone, and the actor admitted that Jennifer had made sure of it: 'It is, because Jennifer bought it and put it on my phone for me,' he revealed.

The song was an instant hit with audiences and critics alike as soon as it was released, but it gathered further momentum after Jared Piccone, aka Spacebrother, remixed it for radio in an up-tempo dance number by DJ Michael Gazzo.

Gazzo told *Entertainment Weekly*: 'Currently topping the charts in almost every single country, the track was a no brainer when it came to remixing!

'My take on "Hanging Tree" is much lighter, and listener-friendly. Although the nature of the track is dark, I envisioned it uplifting an entire group of people to rise up. To unite.'

Jennifer has since struck up a friendship with pop star Lorde, who recorded the official song for the film, 'Yellow Flicker Beat'. The track went on to become so popular that it has won Lorde a nomination for a Golden Globe in the category of Best Original Song. It has also been shortlisted for an Oscar.

In an interview with the *LA Times* in December 2014, Lorde not only described what she went through while composing this song but also revealed that looking at Jennifer's face inspired her most empowering line. The New Zealand born singer talked about the idea behind the composition, saying: 'I liked the idea of the film ending on this close-up of Katniss' face, and then this very creepy, cracked hum kind of signalling your entry into her head, her deepest thoughts and secrets,' she told *The Los Angeles Times*.

She told how she was inspired by a lot of spiritual songs, including 'Sometimes I Feel Like a Motherless Child': 'I wanted the song to feel almost stream-of-consciousness, very much Katniss' innermost thoughts, and when writing it, I could feel the lines blurring, my authorial voice overlapping with hers.'

Lorde also believes that Jennifer's character has so many voices that are both 'internal and external'. She compared her voice to a storm that is not quiet, and quoted her favourite line from her song, which is: 'Fingers laced together and I made a little prison, and I'm locking up everyone who ever laid a finger on me.'

Jennifer may not like to sing, but she may just be the world's most reluctant pop star now.

CHAPTER NINE

STRIKE A POSE

As well as the professional recognition she started receiving from the early days of her career as an actress and a singer, Jennifer was soon also being lauded for her movie-star good looks.

Her fresh-faced appeal and natural curves made her popular with fans, as well as the notoriously hard-to-please fashion world, and lucrative modelling contracts and style accolades began to come her way.

British magazine *Glamour* crowned Jennifer the best-dressed woman in the world in its '50 Best Dressed Women 2014' list. The magazine said that she effortlessly made a Dior gown look as comfortable as sweatpants, and that she somehow pulled off looking equally great in both.

But she has never let the praise go to her head and Jennifer always manages to remain modest about her looks, claiming none of it comes naturally. At one awards show she joked: 'Oh, it takes about four and a half hours and hundreds of dollars and professionals. You too can look like this,' she told *Entertainment Tonight* when asked for details of her red carpet preparations. 'I have an amazing team at Dior and I have a whole pit crew that put their blood, sweat and tears into making me look like this.'

Even when she had her long hair cut into a shoulder-length bob, which sparked headlines across the world, she made a typically self-deprecating joke about how bad it looked, saying: 'It grew to an awkward gross length, and I kept putting it back in a bun and I was like, "I don't want to do this," so I just cut it off,' adding, 'It couldn't get any uglier.'

As a child Jennifer was never particularly girly and so, as stunning as she may appear on the red carpet these days, she found dressing up for glamorous fashion-heavy events awkward and uncomfortable when she first found herself in the public eye: 'I hated dressing up for my first red carpets, because I never felt comfortable in these glamorous dresses,' she told French magazine *Madame Figaro*.

Growing up in Kentucky, she spent her time riding horses and wrestling with her brothers Ben and Blaine, not fawning over fashion magazines and the latest looks.

'In Louisville, when I was a child, I inherited clothes from my two older brothers that I put together with things that my mother dug out of yard sales,' she confessed, adding, 'I was a true tomboy.'

So when she was approached to be the face of Dior – talks began in 2011 and she was offered millions to appear in their global fashion and accessories advertising campaigns for at least the next three years – Jennifer hesitated at first: 'At the beginning I told everyone, "I'm an actress. I'm not a model. I don't want to do it."'

But eventually she agreed, choosing Dior over dozens of other endorsement deals that she was being offered at the time, and she has been under contract to the French luxury house since 2012, when it was announced that she would replace actress Mila Kunis as the face of the Miss Dior handbag line. As well as the $3 million she was paid, Jennifer was also given her pick of the designer's dresses and handbags, which she is seen wearing to almost every high-profile event she attends.

Some of those in the fashion industry were surprised by Dior's choice, as Jennifer had not been known for being particularly on-trend until then, but chief designer Raf Simons said of his choice at the time that he had been stunned by Jennifer: 'Her youth and her classic beauty, but also her force of character and also the feminine strength and complexity she's capable of embodying at such a young age are for me very unique and very appealing.'

Jennifer may not have been the obvious choice at the time, but gradually she has settled into her role as a high-profile spokesmodel. 'Now I get the haute couture thing,' she explained later. 'It's a big deal. I don't know what "haute" means, but I have to say it.

'It is only recently that I discovered the beauty of haute couture. The first Dior collection I attended by Raf Simons blew me away.'

When the first set of campaign shots, taken by legendary fashion photographer Patrick Demarchelier, were released in 2013, Jennifer looked amazing. But she was suitably modest when it emerged that the photos had been controversially retouched to enhance her figure – Dior was accused of digitally altering Jennifer's shoulders to make them appear drastically narrower in a campaign.

But while many critics were outraged by the move, Jennifer herself was delighted, and she told *Access Hollywood*: 'I love Photoshop more than anything in the world. Of course it's Photoshop – people don't look like that.'

Now, despite her jokes, wearing high fashion has become second nature to Jennifer, and, like many other women, she has even found herself unable to live without an oversized purse on her arm: 'I have an enormous one, nicknamed "The Flagship", which I lug around everywhere and everything is in there,' she admitted. 'My basics? Lollipops for my nephews, my wallet, my passport, my phone, and a collection of lip balms and pens. Since they always fall to the bottom, I forget and buy new ones, non-stop.'

In another campaign for Be Dior, launched in February 2015, Jennifer looked stunning in the photos by Paolo Roversi, but admitted that she is surprisingly very low maintenance for a movie star who has reluctantly become a style icon. Asked again what she keeps in her designer handbag, she told *Woman's Wear Daily*: 'Wallet, phone, keys – if I can remember them – ChapStick and a little perfume.'

The pictures also caused amusement since Jennifer could be

seen relaxing on a white staircase, and the *New York Post* joked: 'It's been two years since Jennifer Lawrence's infamous trip on the stairs at the Academy Awards in her Dior gown – and the actress is finally ready to conquer the steps once and for all in the brand's Spring/Summer 2015 campaign.'

The official Dior website also raved about the photos, saying: 'An architecturally pure and minimalist location was the one chosen by Italian photographer Paolo Roversi as the perfect setting for a series of portraits in which he sought to capture the natural aura of Jennifer Lawrence, the Oscar-winning Christian Dior muse.'

By this time she was being taken so seriously by the fashion elite it was announced Jennifer would co-chair the glitziest event in the style calendar: the Met Gala in May 2015. 'Chinese Whispers' was the theme for the annual ball: Tales of the East in Art, Film and Fashion. US *Vogue* editor-in-chief Anna Wintour, Chinese actress Gong Li, Wendi Murdoch (former wife of the newspaper magnate) and *Yahoo!* CEO Marissa Mayer would be joining Jennifer in the co-chairing duties for the event, which is always attended by a galaxy of A-list stars.

The previous year, *Sex and the City* star Sarah Jessica Parker and Jennifer's favourite co-star Bradley Cooper had co-chaired the annual red carpet extravaganza.

Part of Jennifer's huge popularity has been put down to the fact that she appears to have such a normal attitude to her body, and her decision to avoid extreme diets and food fads, and to steer completely clear of plastic surgery or the latest beauty crazes has endeared her to millions.

She has a naturally toned figure, and does not appear super-skinny, like so many Hollywood actresses. While other stars subject themselves to punishing diets and gruelling workout regimes, Jennifer has spoken out many times about how she refuses to bow to pressure to lose weight for a role, and is refreshingly honest, especially by celebrity standards, when she openly admits that she actually enjoys eating junk food and drinking alcohol.

A self-confessed lover of junk food, including pizza and burgers, she once revealed how she was told she would not get an acting job unless she immediately went on a diet to lose a few pounds, to which she replied: 'You can go fuck yourself.'

Indeed Jennifer often talks happily about her healthy appetite and love of food. In an interview alongside Liam Hemsworth she once recalled: 'Do you remember that one time I was at your house and we ate a whole pizza and then I stopped at McDonald's and got a double quarter pounder?

'Then I passed out in a food coma and a ketchup packet stuck to my ass.'

She has also revealed a love of unhealthy snacks, which is a rare admission in body-conscious Hollywood: 'Cool Ranch Doritos are my girl. I've been trying to wean myself off Cool Ranch Doritos and move on to Pirate's Booty [snack food]. It's just not doing the trick,' she grinned.

This refreshing attitude to eating has led to Jennifer being seen as a positive role model for young girls wanting to break into show business without having to resort to drastic measures to alter their appearances. She is all too aware of the impact her words have on vulnerable young girls who aspire to be like her, so she makes sure she chooses carefully, and is always keen to advocate a healthy attitude to diet and exercise. 'There's that Kate Moss quote that nothing tastes as good as skinny feels,' she said. 'I can name a lot of things that taste better than skinny feels – potatoes, bread, Philly cheesesteak and fries.

'We see these unobtainable perfect bodies and that's what we are comparing ourselves to. I would rather look chubby on screen and like a person in real life.'

Although she jokes about her passion for eating and drinking whatever she likes, Jennifer has also spoken out about how furious it makes her when women are labelled fat. 'Because why is humiliating people funny? I get it and I do it too, we all do it,' she told Barbara Walters in a frank TV interview in December 2013. 'But I think when it comes to the media, the media needs to take responsibility for the effect it has on our younger generation, on these girls who are watching these television shows, and picking up how to talk and how to be cool.

'So then all of a sudden being funny is making fun of the girl that's wearing an ugly dress – and the word fat. I just think it should be illegal to call somebody fat on TV.

'If we're regulating cigarettes and sex and cuss words because of the effect they have on our younger generation, why aren't we regulating things like calling people fat?'

Jennifer has never forgotten the first time she encountered that attitude. 'I was young,' she told *Bazaar* magazine. 'It was just the kind of stuff that actresses have to go through. Somebody told me I was fat, that I was going to get fired if I didn't lose a certain amount of weight. Someone brought it up recently, they thought that because of the way my career had gone, it wouldn't still hurt me. That somehow, after I won an Oscar, I'm above it all. "You really still care about that?" Yeah, I was a little girl. I was hurt. It doesn't matter what accolades you get.'

While she herself certainly has never appeared chubby, and landed several modelling jobs as a teenager, thanks to her toned and athletic-looking figure, she admits that she has always been too curvy to be taken seriously as a catwalk model in the fashion world. 'I always ate too much to be a model,' she said. 'Food is one of my favourite parts of the day.'

And unlike many of her contemporaries, Jennifer has no problem admitting that she drinks alcohol – and is often spotted sipping wine or cocktails. When asked by *Marie Claire* magazine how she was going to prepare for a 4am start she joked: 'I'm going to have a bottle of red wine tonight.'

And in a later interview with *Yahoo* she added that strict diets to conform to stereotypes have never been on her agenda: 'What are you going to do? Be hungry every single day to make other people happy? That's just dumb.

'I'm really sick of all these actresses looking like birds.'

While growing up, Jennifer experienced eating disorders and vowed to be more sensible. 'I'm just so sick of these young girls with diets,' she told *Seventeen*. 'I remember when I was thirteen and it was cool to pretend to have an eating disorder because there were rumours that Lindsay Lohan and Nicole Richie were anorexic. I thought it was crazy. I went home and told my mom, "Nobody's eating bread – I just had to finish everyone's burgers!"'

For her role as Katniss in *The Hunger Games*, Jennifer was required to be at the peak of physical fitness to have the high levels of stamina required to perform difficult stunts and skills. In the run-up to filming she had to follow a series of stringent workouts to ensure she would be flexible and strong enough for the demanding role, but losing weight was not on the agenda.

A routine exercise plan was laid out to ensure she was physically and mentally fit enough, so she hired an expert personal trailer to keep her routine on track. Dr Joe Horrigan, who specialises in chiropractic sports medicine, is always in huge demand in Hollywood, having previously worked with many other big name stars.

He set up a specific exercise plan that was moulded to fit Jennifer's style and habits. According to Horrigan, the actress's exercise model was composed of five parts. Her regular workout included cardio, strength training, yoga, routine and attitude training, all designed to prepare her for the running and fight scenes that were required in the script.

Dr Horrigan told *Teen Vogue* that strength training was a big part of the process. But rather than relying on weights alone, he encouraged Jennifer to endure a routine consisting of 'bodyweight squats, push-ups, and sit-ups all performed in a circuit'.

He added: 'If you can do any of these exercises for 20 minutes at high intensity, you will see results.

'Jennifer was never late. She never missed a workout. She never complained. She did everything that was asked of her and she usually did so with a smile.'

However, Jennifer argued that she didn't really enjoy the workouts, saying she only did them because she had to for the job: 'I hate saying I like exercising – I want to punch people who say that in the face,' she told US *OK!* magazine. 'Sometimes I exercise – but I never want to be one of those people who says, "I just don't feel good unless I don't work out"! I just watch reality TV. I love *The Real Housewives*, *Intervention* and I'm obsessed with *Shark Tank*.

'I am keeping up! I am always keeping up. I do exercise! You can't work when you're hungry, you know?'

She told *Elle* magazine that when preparing for the role she was conscious about looking 'fit and strong – not thin and underfed', especially with so many young women watching closely, and wanting to emulate her look: 'I run, I do yoga and stuff like that but it's not what I do every day. If I don't have anything to do all day I might not even put my pants [trousers] on.'

Even though Jennifer has joked that by Hollywood standards she is an 'obese' actress who can find nothing to motivate her to work out, she is always happy to be put through her paces to prepare for upcoming films that require her to be in healthy-looking shape, and she would always rather exercise than deprive herself of her favourite foods: 'In Hollywood I'm

obese, I'm never going to starve myself for a part,' she told *Elle*.
'I keep waiting for that one role to come along that scares me
enough into dieting, and it just can't happen. I'm invincible.

'I don't want little girls to be like, "Oh, I want to look like
Katniss, so I'm going to skip dinner." That's something I was
really conscious of during training, when you're trying to get
your body to look exactly right. I was trying to get my body
to look fit and strong – not thin and underfed. I'll be the only
actress who doesn't have anorexia rumours.'

Jennifer is always concerned that her fans will copy her, and
has given words of advice when asked how to follow in her
footsteps: 'Be strong. Don't be a follower, and always do the
right thing,' she said in an interview with *Parade* magazine.
'If you have a choice between the right thing and the wrong
thing, the right way is always the less stressful.'

Nevertheless, plus-size model Ashley Graham, who has
appeared in *Vogue* and *Elle*, lambasted Hollywood's treatment
of women's bodies in an essay for Net-a-Porter's online
magazine, *The Edit*, suggesting it was ridiculous that someone
as slim as Jennifer Lawrence should be considered curvy. The
model, who is a UK size 14, wrote: 'I think that you can be
healthy at any size and my goal is to help and educate women
on that. It doesn't matter if you're a size two or 22 as long
as you're taking care of your body, working out, and telling
yourself, "I love you" instead of taking in the negativity of
beauty standards.'

Though she acknowledged that Hollywood starlets like
Marilyn Monroe and Jennifer Lopez have worn their curves

with confidence over the years, Graham went on to say that she believes girls need to see more women on TV and in magazines with healthy figures: 'Young girls don't have much to look at, curvy women are not on covers of magazines, they're not talked about on social media as much as other celebrities. Jennifer Lawrence is the media's poster girl for curves – she's tiny!'

Many commentators have made a point of highlighting the massive difference between Jennifer – who loves meat, sugar and alcohol – and Chris Martin's ex, Gwyneth Paltrow, who is known for following a strict macrobiotic and gluten-free diet. And so it caused quite a storm when Jennifer was somewhat dismissive of precisely those food intolerances in an interview with *Vanity Fair*. 'The gluten-free diet is the new, cool eating disorder, the "basically I just don't eat carbs,"' she said.

And the gluten-free community was none too thrilled by Jennifer's comments either: 'Being gluten-free is not an eating disorder,' Cynthia Kupper, executive director for the Gluten Intolerance Group and a registered dietician, told *FOX411*. 'When I think of an eating disorder, I think anorexia, bulimia or strange eating patterns. Jennifer's comments make me angry.'

In the photo shoot that accompanied the *Vanity Fair* interview and which took place at a private mansion in the Hollywood Hills, Jennifer proved she has no hang-ups about her body as she revealed almost every inch of it when she posed covered by nothing but a snake. She fearlessly stripped naked for the revealing photos by Patrick Demarchelier and apparently did not flinch at the idea of being draped in a giant – and strategically placed – Colombian red-tailed boa constrictor, somehow managing to remain relaxed throughout.

In the sexy images, Jennifer can be seen lying on her stomach, her feet pointing in the air and her back arched, while being covered by a boa constrictor that is draped across her neck.

As always, she looked flawless and had an air of old-school Hollywood glamour, with curled hair and a smouldering look. It was considered to be her most provocative shoot to date, especially coming so soon after she had complained about nude photos of herself being seen by millions in the hacking scandal.

'Jennifer has the perfect combination of strength, sexuality, and humor, and, above all, tomboy to pull this off,' explained shoot stylist Jessica Diehl.

Apparently the actress only expressed discomfort when the snake began to coil more closely to her, after which it was returned to a perforated storage container. Luckily, she is not afraid of snakes. When asked about her greatest fear she replied: 'Spiders, I'm very afraid of spiders – and ghosts. I wouldn't say I'm as afraid of ghosts as I am paranoid of ghosts.'

The shot is in homage to the iconic 1981 portrait of Nastassja Kinski, taken by photographer Richard Avedon for *Vogue* magazine. Entitled 'Nastassja Kinski and the Serpent', the shot captured the naked actress adopting a similar pose as the serpent, an enormous Burmese python, worked its way across her back. Avedon's image was later marketed as a poster and sold across the world. The original eventually sold at auction for $74,500 in 2014.

Jennifer's raunchy shoot was part of *Vanity Fair*'s annual Hollywood issue, which also featured a number of British Oscar nominees such as David Oyelowo, Felicity Jones, Benedict Cumberbatch and Best Actor winner Eddie Redmayne.

As well as having a coveted figure, Jennifer has also become much admired for her beautiful face and flawless complexion. Her skincare facialist Sonya Dakar has told how she is very strict with the actress, but Jennifer loves her for it. In the run-up to high-profile events, Sonya devises a six-week beauty boot camp for Jennifer, to ensure her skin is red carpet ready.

She issues the actress with skin-perfecting beauty tips to ensure a mega-watt glow, and says: 'If you follow these tips there's no way on the planet you are not going to look years younger, sexier, healthier, and more beautiful.'

Unlike many other stars, Jennifer has not yet dared inject her face with Botox or fillers. Sonya explains why she herself has banned them: 'My philosophy and my concept means there is no way clients can go get injectables and then ask me to make it more natural.

'So I put my foot down and say, "You cannot do anything like this." I don't care who the client is. I don't care if it's Queen Elizabeth. At that point, it is ten steps forward and nine backwards. Absolutely not! It has to be me alone with my work and my technology.'

Working with Jennifer, Sonya says she has seen first-hand the link between diet, exercise and healthy skin – 'I tell clients, drink water and watch your diet. Be super gluten-free for the week of the Oscars, stay away from bulky food, and please exercise.'

Several weeks before Jennifer is due to appear at an event, Sonya works on ridding her skin of any problems, and one of her favourite treatments is the Diamond Peel: 'It is sixteen different diamond-tipped wands focusing on texture. What it does is resurface, remove lines, and acne on face, neck and chest. I also do arms because a lot of my celebrities wear beautiful gowns.'

Jennifer also has regular facials, using a variety of techniques to transform her skin, including radio frequency, LED lights and even stem cells. 'The stem cells come from a rare Swiss apple and offer specific benefit – getting rid of all the pores, anti-aging and making skin flawless,' added Sonya.

She also warns the actress not to have any extreme treatments before the main event, which could cause raw, red skin. Jennifer usually has her last treatment forty-eight hours before walking down the red carpet: 'Two days before, I do the red light LED, some oxygen and a light peel,' Sonya said. 'I will not take a risk, not even a tiny risk. It has to be gorgeous when you walk out. You'll be camera-ready from the second you leave here.'

Serums and oils add an extra glow to the actress's skin:

'The liquid gold omega serum is the magic secret weapon. Before make-up, they just use two drops and tap it into skin.

'The secret is to do your homework. My clients have seven to eight products they have to use every single night – masks, flash facials, moisturisers,' she explained. 'You cannot change your face for the better, unless you take care of it every day.'

While she is clearly at the peak of her style and beauty, Jennifer admitted in an interview with *Us Weekly* that she was still far from confident about her looks or her onscreen success. 'I'm constantly waiting for things to fall apart,' she said about her unexpected popularity. 'Every time the phone rings, I'm like, "It's over!"' But despite her doubts, she was named the Sexiest Woman in the World 2014 by men's magazine *FHM*. She was also included in lists of the best bodies by lingerie giant Victoria's Secret, being named as the celebrity with the sexiest hair in 2014 and sexiest eyes in 2012.

Esquire magazine named her The Best Celebrity for its October 2013 issue as it celebrated its 80th anniversary. And she and football star David Beckham were named as the two most desired celebrities to have a selfie with on Valentine's Day, according to a survey. Smartphone giant HTC asked 2,000 UK residents who they would most like to take a photo of themselves with, and the most desirable female was Jennifer, beating off competition from pop stars Rihanna and Katy Perry to take the top spot. The highest-placed Brit on the female list was Kelly Brook in sixth place.

Those surveyed were also asked to name the famous selfie they would most like to recreate, with Ellen DeGeneres' celebrated Oscar selfie – which of course included Jennifer, alongside the likes of Brad Pitt, Angelina Jolie and Kevin Spacey – coming out on top. Taken in February 2014, the famous photo got a record 779,295 re-tweets on Twitter in the first half hour alone, causing the social media site to temporarily crash.

That selfie, which also featured Bradley Cooper, Julia Roberts and Meryl Streep, was chosen ahead of Germany striker Lukas Podolski's World Cup selfie of the German team all shirtless in the changing room following a match, and model Cara Delevingne's 'ugly' shot in which she contorted her normally beautiful face by making goofy cross eyes and a turned-up pig nose!

Jennifer has explained that her young fans would rather take a selfie than have an autograph, and according to statistics, the selfie is a still-growing craze, with an estimated 11 million eighteen- to thirty-year-olds posting selfies in 2014, making up more than a billion in total. The average person in that age group takes 100 selfies a year, posting at least one a week to social media.

But the art of the selfie was dealt a blow in April 2015 when the organisers of the prestigious Cannes Film Festival tried to ban selfies on the red carpet, branding them 'ridiculous and grotesque'. One organiser added: 'Honestly, you're never as ugly as on a selfie.'

It's no wonder, then, that the results show that the humble autograph no longer interests celebrity spotters, with over half of those asked (55 per cent) saying they would choose having a selfie with their favourite celebrity over anything else, with only 22 per cent saying they would ask for an autograph. A third of men said they would ask their celebrity crush on a date or for a kiss if they met them, while only 11 per cent of women said the same.

On top of all this, Jennifer was so enduringly popular that she was named the most-searched-for celebrity of 2014 by Google. While many thought that reality star Kim Kardashian would top the poll, following her naked photo shoot for *Paper* magazine that was entitled 'Break the Internet', Jennifer was the surprise winner.

And every time she tries out a new style or even gets a haircut, it makes headlines. In early 2014, when she had her trademark blonde mane cut into a stylish cropped pixie bob, photos were beamed around the world, and the look was immediately copied by thousands of women.

Even Victoria's Secret model Karlie Kloss confessed that she was jealous, and wished she could change her style as effortlessly as Jennifer. 'I thought Jennifer Lawrence looked amazing when she cut her hair short. I'm always envious when anyone tries out a new style,' she explained.

Scores of celebrity admirers and professional critics appear utterly devoted to the actress, admiring every fashion choice and style selection she makes. And it seems Jennifer can only get more and more popular as she matures into a sophisticated young woman, gradually becoming ever more confident as she gets used to living this extraordinary life under the glare of the spotlight.

CHAPTER TEN

PLAYING
THE FOOL

Unlike most movie stars, who carefully stage-manage every word and deed to ensure a purely positive public perception, Jennifer does not seem to care about saying and doing the wrong thing. By messing up, telling embarrassing stories and often saying exactly what she thinks without a thought for the consequences, she has shown the world that she is still enchantingly natural and down to earth.

Of course there are those who would argue that as she is now one of the most in-demand actresses in the world, nothing she says or does is accidental, and surely it must all be an act, but there is no doubt Jennifer loves to laugh at herself and seems to have barely changed since she first shot to fame with an Oscar nomination for her role in the low-budget indie flick *Winter's Bone* in 2011.

Since then she has become so notorious for her gaffes, trips, falls and photobombing that she even made a joke out of her quirky reputation when she had to make a speech at the Producers Guild Awards in January 2015. She had been asked to present Lionsgate CEO Jon Feltheimer with the illustrious Milestone Award.

The only problem was that – despite being a professional actress – Jennifer does not really like giving speeches due to what she describes as her 'crippling anxiety', which is why she normally turns down requests to make unscripted speeches.

'When I heard it was for Feltheimer, I had to say yes,' she explained, 'because I just assumed that I was contractually obligated. When I found out that I wasn't, I had already picked out this dress.'

She then warned Feltheimer: 'I know what you're thinking, I'm going to totally mess this up – and you're right.'

The Academy Award-winning actress did not mess up, though. Instead she had the audience in stitches right from her opening remark about wishing she had thought to ask one of them for a Xanax to calm her nerves, and mentioning 'the unbreakable bond between woman and couch'.

She even managed to tease the studio head behind the wildly popular *The Hunger Games* movies. 'Jon was charged to insure that Suzanne Collins' *Hunger Games* incredible trilogy of books was respectfully brought to life in four films and it was a large fucking failure!' she joked. 'I was so afraid of signing on to these movies a few years ago because something that size can make or break a career,' she went on.

'I put my trust in Lionsgate and they put their trust in me

and now I think we have a strong and amazing relationship that I hope lasts until my career dies at thirty-five.'

While that seems highly unlikely, if her career does peter out, Jennifer can undoubtedly make a living as a toastmaster. On set, she has a reputation for getting the giggles, no matter how serious the scene may be: 'That's not because I'm funny,' she explained. 'I'm just really immature and I can't be serious for long or it kills me. Especially if we're doing an emotional scene, I just can't be serious.'

In April 2015 she took part in an elaborate April Fool's Day stunt to promote a revolutionary 1.5-second looping video site called *Dips*. Alongside big-name stars, including Britney Spears and Ashton Kutcher, she filmed a short clip for the new start-up site, said to be worth a staggering $80 million, which shares 'blink-of-an-eye' clips hosted by Funny Or Die, a comedy video company founded by Will Ferrell and Adam McKay. In her clip, Jennifer looked bedraggled and was seen answering a banana instead of a phone.

Indeed she has become almost as famous for her sense of humour as her acting roles, and being able to laugh at herself. When asked in 2012 about the dance moves she would have to showcase in *Silver Linings Playbook* she said: 'When I dance, I look like I'm a dad at a prom. I never grasped my limbs. Ever since puberty I've just kind of felt like we don't understand each other.'

Jennifer often pokes fun at her own looks too. She has been snapped combing her hair with a fork and sticking her finger up the nose of giant billboard photos of herself. In one red carpet interview she rearranged her strapless dress in an unladylike way, explaining: 'I know, I have armpit fat, it's OK, though. Armpit vagina, it's awful! I see myself in all these cameras, it's awful! I need to wear like horse shades so I can't see anything.

'So what dress are you wearing? Sorry, Dior! You asked me and all I talked about was vaginas!'

She admits she can mess up in live interviews because she finds being on the red carpet so stressful. 'Red carpets are so scary,' she said. 'I end up getting so nervous that I get hyper. So I go into interviews and I'm like, "I'm a Chihuahua! I'm shaking and peeing!" And then afterward, I'm like, "I just talked about peeing on the red carpet!"'

Her friend Josh Hutcherson joked about her famous fall at the Oscars before he made his own debut at the ceremony, two years later. When it was suggested that he should have asked Jennifer for advice, considering how many times his co-star had attended the ceremony, he replied: 'I don't want to ask her any advice about the Oscars. I'm staying away from that train wreck, for sure.'

At unite4:good's unite4:humanity gala in 2015, where he was honoured for his work with gay rights group, Straight But Not Narrow, Josh took Jennifer as his date, describing her as his best friend, and joked about her being much taller than him, saying: 'I don't have heels. I'm not busting out the heels for this one.'

Josh and Jennifer have become known for their fun friend-ship – on the set of *The Hunger Games* he even nicknamed her

Katpiss Neverclean because of the sweaty workouts she was forced to endure twice a day while filming to keep in shape for the role.

But Josh told *Vanity Fair* they will always be close: 'It's been the most incredible experience making these movies. I've made friends that I'm going to have forever. Nothing is as bonding or as close an experience as filming a movie with someone. I'm going to miss that closeness, for sure.'

He added that he, Jennifer and Liam have promised to reunite at least once every two years for a 'group vacation lasting four to eight days'.

As well as endearing her to a legion of fans, Jennifer's good humour has earned her a somewhat varied selection of famous admirers too. She was left blushing when Hollywood legend Jack Nicholson congratulated her on scooping the Oscar. And Bradley Cooper told *Press Association* at the 58th BFI London Film Festival that he couldn't have asked for a better co-star after they appeared in several films together, saying: 'I've sort of hit the jackpot with being able to work with Jennifer Lawrence on *Silver Linings Playbook*. When I knew she was going to play this character, I was fully aware it was going to be comic.

'Once she would breathe life into this character, it would become much more dimensional. It could be very easy to portray her as a stock character and there's just not one moment where you don't believe she's a human being.'

And he heaped more praise on his favourite co-star, adding: 'She's a wonderful, wonderful actress.

'Her biggest asset is probably her level of relaxation when she acts, and because of that, it's a very thrilling thing to be involved with as the partner of the scene.'

Jennifer added that the thing they share most in common is their love of food: 'We're two of the biggest eaters in Hollywood!' she admitted.

But despite their relationship being described as strictly platonic, Bradley continued to gush about his co-star at the event, saying: 'I respect her so much as a professional, as an actor, and I think she's the best there is. I just learn from her. You always want to work with people who are better than you.'

And making it clear that there is a solid connection between the two, Jennifer added: 'And I feel the same way about him.' She even playfully stroked her leading man's cheek as he laughed and squinted while posing for pictures at the after-party.

Jennifer has many other big-name admirers – she was even compared to Jesus and Joan of Arc by her *Hunger Games* co-star Donald Sutherland: 'When I worked with her, I realised the child was a genius,' he said at the premiere of *Mockingjay Part 1*. 'She's the right person at the right time in the sense of Joan of Arc or Jesus Christ, any genius, in that sense.

'She has the ability as an actor to tell the truth out of the material, and that truth is immediately recognisable with everybody because it hits you in your heart, your solar plexus and your mind. And she has the genius of person to be not affected by all of this. She's just a real girl.'

Sutherland even compared Jennifer to legendary actor Sir Laurence Olivier, describing her as 'an exquisite and brilliant actress'.

But Jennifer is typically modest about all the praise lavished upon her, and is often humble enough to bring up the fact that she has never studied acting at all, and that her way of learning 'method' acting has been to simply watch people's expressions and emotions, adding that she has always been fascinated by the reactions and feelings that others express around her. She has said: 'Watching people is the best acting class you can take.'

Another of Jennifer's *Hunger Games* co-stars, Woody Harrelson, also praised her, saying that she has not allowed fame to go to her head, and has remained down to earth despite becoming the 'biggest female star in the world'. Recalling the first time they ever met, Woody told *Vanity Fair* magazine: 'She'd just done a movie, and people in the industry knew her, but she wasn't really famous. And so I watched her grow into, amazingly, the biggest female star in the world.

'And it's staggering to me how much she's been able to just hold on to her basic decency and her amazing, marvellous spirit. You know, it's not terrible, people tell you you're great; what's terrible is when you start believing it. She never got fucked up.

'She's an amazing girl. She's one of my favourite people on the planet, and I can't imagine my life without her.'

Woody has also told how he delights in the fact that his friend has no filter and never worries about censoring herself: 'She's just very forthcoming. It's almost shocking how much she'll say, you know. That's super-fun, and also it's shocking sometimes because it's so on the edge,' he added. 'It's like she doesn't have a censor. I really love that in people. I guess there are some people I don't love it in, but in her it's wonderful.'

'When I think about the fact that I did turn down *The Hunger Games* at first and had to be talked into it by director Gary Ross, I think to myself the thing that I would miss more than anything – you know, certainly, I'd want to be a part of *The Hunger Games* just generally in the other aspects – but not getting to know Jen is just, like, inconceivable.'

Jennifer made quite an impression the first time she met Harrelson: as she walked into his trailer, she looked over at his yoga exercise swing and said: 'Hi Woody, is that a sex swing?'

He added: 'Jennifer doesn't have a trace of arrogance. She's not trying to put on any airs or be anyone she's not. She's the real deal.

'She's just this frickin' amazing girl from Kentucky who hit it big.'

Another *Hunger Games* co-star, teenage actress Willow Shields, also told how much she has enjoyed growing up with Jennifer Lawrence as her on-screen sister. 'She's pretty much an open book. She's herself in interviews and she's herself on red carpets, so it's not like there is anything that surprising about her,' said Willow. 'I feel like some people just see the funny side of her, but she can be a very serious and sophisticated person, and I think that's something a lot of people don't know.'

And when Willow appeared as a contestant on *Dancing with the Stars*, she told how Jennifer admired her bravery, dancing in public. 'I think everybody is like, "Where did this come from? Oh my God, you're dancing,"' Willow told *E! News*. 'Like Jen, of course she was like, "Oh God, I would be so scared to do that." They're all very excited.'

Willow went on to tell *Access Hollywood* how she feels she has grown up with Jennifer. 'She's awesome,' said the young actress. 'I started when I was ten. Now, I'm fourteen. We built this fantastic relationship. Each movie we grew closer, so we're like sisters now and she's so supportive of everything I do.
'She told me to stay who I am. I think she knew that these films were going to just blow up and I didn't yet. I was ten and I was totally unaware of what was going to happen, so for me I had no idea,' Willow continued. 'She was like, stay who you are. The only way you're going to be successful in this industry is to kind of be humble and stay who you are because obviously they cast you for a reason.

'She's an inspiration to me. She's never changed this entire series, which is the most incredible thing you can see. The way she stays so grounded and humble, it's almost impossible for a lot of people to do that, so for me it's inspirational,' she added. 'She's such an inspiration for every young girl out there.'

Jennifer's other famous fans include Julianne Moore, who revealed how much they had laughed the first time she met her *Hunger Games* co-star: 'She's very funny. When I first met her, I was sitting in the make-up trailer, and our make-up artist was testing something, and Jennifer came in. I said, "Oh, let me get up." She goes, "No, no, no. You sit there. And I'll secretly resent you."'

Meanwhile, when *Harry Potter* star Daniel Radcliffe was asked which actors he admires said: 'George Clooney, Jennifer Lawrence, I just think they'd be really cool. Paul Rudd, I met him and was like, "You're awesome!" I just want to work with people you can get on with, and you have a good rapport with, and those are definitely some of them.'

And the feeling is mutual. Jennifer described the first time she met Daniel: 'I screamed at him the first time that I met him.'

And he is not the only one longing to work alongside Jennifer. The team behind the hugely popular US teen drama *Pretty Little Liars* – which has a very intense and dedicated army of fans who twect and talk about the plot twists more than almost any other show – would like to get Jennifer on board.

Although the complicated storylines and near-death experiences keep the viewing figures high and ensure audiences stay loyal, the show's breakout star, Keegan Allen (Toby Cavanaugh), is keen to attract high-profile guest stars, and described Jennifer as an alpha female: 'It would be really cool to work with Jennifer Lawrence. I'm so often reminded of Jennifer Lawrence by Troian [Bellisario, who plays Spencer]. She feels like that alpha female presence – I mean, all the girls are very alpha female – and it would be cool to have her come on the show. Or even Taylor Swift! There's an element of that alpha female in the vibe I get from both of those girls, and our fan base would love that. But it would also be cool to see their take on a character coming into that world.'

Allen even admitted he had a plot line mapped out if ever he managed to convince Jennifer to make the move into TV drama: 'I feel like Jennifer Lawrence could be an opposing debate team member against Spencer and be really, really good at it, and Spencer gets freaked out a bit because this girl is smart and competing to get into some crazy Ivy League college or something,' he added excitedly. 'And then Taylor Swift's character could be this lacrosse-playing, super-athletic cool girl that comes in and can play guitar as well. She makes Aria really jealous or something.'

Ultimately, he said he saw the two stars as foes that turn into friends, rather than straight-up allies in the beginning. The Liars have to earn their trust, after all, and then they can all team up. 'Bringing them in, the conflict would be more fun than having them as allies to start,' he explained. 'And then they become allies. It would start as a conflict and then change.'

In fact, he said he was so excited by the idea that he wanted to pitch it to the show's creator, Marlene King: 'See what you're doing now? Now I'm all into this and I'm going to get off the phone and go, "Marlene! Let's get Taylor Swift and Jennifer Lawrence on the show!"'

Yet another of Jennifer's *Hunger Games* co-stars, British actor Toby Jones, has also told how inspiring he found working with her. 'I've worked with Jennifer on other films and it's so interesting because she's such a smart, clever actress,' he said. 'You'd think there would be a danger of it swamping her but it never does.'

Megan Fox also loves the candid and goofy actress, labelling Jen a 'fearless female'.

'I definitely think she's ruling the world right now,' she told the *Daily News*.

And Academy Award–winning French star Marion Cotillard has enjoyed hanging out with the 'fun' star too – together they have been muses for Dior. When asked by *Stylist* magazine who makes her laugh the most right now, Marion replied: 'Will Ferrell! My friends. I have very, very funny friends. They make me laugh because I laugh so hard. Oh, and Jennifer Lawrence. Yeah, that's a good list.

'I have a Dior dinner, which I'm looking forward to because they're amazing, funny people. And Jennifer Lawrence will be there so I'm going to have a lot of fun.'

Patrick Stewart has nothing but praise for her, either. The *Star Trek* veteran has worked with an endless number of talented actors and actresses over the years. With a lengthy résumé, and notable connections, Stewart has had the opportunity to work with pretty much anyone he pleases. But while promoting his film, *Match* (2015), the actor was asked who he would most like to collaborate with in the future, and he chose Jennifer because of her brilliant sense of humour.

He saw her in action when the pair starred alongside each other in *X-Men: Days of Future Past*, but they never actually got to work together since Stewart's character lived in the future time of the film, while Jennifer's existed in the past. Although they never shared a scene, he was still very impressed by what he saw.

In an *Entertainment Weekly* question and answer session on Facebook, Stewart said: 'I'd like to collaborate with Jennifer Lawrence. I think she's brilliant, with a great sense of humour, and quite good looking.'

WWE Superstar Seth Rollins also has a crush on Jennifer and would like to film some romantic scenes with her. The famous wrestler said he enjoyed watching her in *The Hunger Games* franchise, and would love to follow in the footsteps of his WWE alumni Dwayne 'The Rock' Johnson and Dave Bautista – who had recently been cast as henchman Mr Hinx in the new James Bond movie *Spectre* – and make the move into Hollywood, if it meant he would get the chance to work with Jennifer.

Rollins said: 'If the opportunity presents itself to go into acting, I definitely wouldn't turn it down. I wouldn't mind doing some romantic scenes with some beautiful leading ladies.

'Man, who is my favourite? That's a tough one, man, there are so many wonderful and beautiful leading ladies, but I'd say Jennifer Lawrence. She's looking mighty good in *The Hunger Games* trilogy. We'll see if that can happen.'

Project Runway champion Dmitry Sholokhov declared after winning the hit TV show in April 2015 that his dream would be to dress Jennifer. 'I'd love to dress Jennifer Lawrence, Tilda Swinton and Angelina Jolie,' he told *Hollywood Life*. 'Those particular celebrities have a very particular style, strong aesthetics, and it's interesting to work with women who are not afraid to take risks and not afraid to be different.'

It was even suggested that Prince Harry wanted to date Jennifer, but she turned down the chance to possibly become a member of the British Royal family. Apparently, when Jennifer was in London promoting *Mockingjay – Part 1* in November 2014, Harry tried to use his illustrious position to land a date.

Life and Style magazine reported: 'Harry made his aide invite her out to dinner and coupled it with an invite for her to see Kensington Palace.'

But it later emerged that Jennifer was not interested and politely turned Harry's invitation down.

Not everybody loves Jennifer with quite so much enthusiasm, though. Actor, writer and director Ethan Hawke has said he believes her career peaked way too early. And he thinks that winning an Oscar at such a young age would only work against her.

He does not think that landing at the top of *Forbes*' list of bankable stars of 2014 is something to rejoice about either. 'I feel sorry for a young actress like Jennifer Lawrence who gets so much success out of the gate, because how are you supposed to develop an appropriate work ethic? How do you push yourself to be better when you get an Oscar for buying breakfast in the morning?' he told *The Daily Beast*, adding that early success can have a negative effect on a person's work ethic and motivation.

Hawke quoted a Tennessee Williams' essay called 'The Catastrophe of Success', explaining that failure and success can both turn out to be negative experiences – but failure can fuel a person to be better, while success might ultimately drown them.

He went on to say that it is the way Hollywood runs as a whole that's the problem. In his view the industry has a culture that decides when something is brilliant, even though it may not be.

Actress Chloë Scvigny also admitted that she is not among Jennifer's huge army of fans, either. In an interview with *V* magazine in March 2015, she slammed her as annoying and crass.

'I love when a movie star is a great movie star,' Sevigny explained. 'I think Angelina is a great movie star. I like Emma Stone. Whenever she's herself, she's really cute. Jennifer Lawrence I find annoying. Too crass.'

The star of *The Kids* added: 'I'm afraid that maybe people think there's more personality than acting ability. So much is about marketing and selling the product.

'They'll have a really peppy funny girl on the talk show rounds, and everybody adores her and loves her and wants to be her or fuck her, and then so many more people want to watch the movie of the TV show. I understand that star quality, how much value that carries.'

Despite the harsh criticism, Jennifer resisted sinking into a slanging match with her critics, preferring to remain silent on the matter, as she so often does – despite being urged to retort!

Regardless of praise or condemnation, she does her best to ignore the majority of public opinion and relies instead on her close-knit family and trusted friends to keep her feet on the ground and tell her the truth: 'I tell my friends to slap me if they ever think I'm getting full of myself!'

CHAPTER ELEVEN

LOVE IS
IN THE AIR

Since becoming world famous, Jennifer has found her love life very firmly under the spotlight, with her every move analysed, dissected, discussed and critiqued just as much – if not more – than her movie roles.

In 2011 she started dating British actor Nicholas Hoult, who first found fame as the nerdy kid who strikes up an unlikely friendship with Hugh Grant's carefree bachelor character in *About a Boy* (2002). Jennifer and Nicholas met on the set of *X-Men: First Class* in 2010, where he played the character Beast, and sparks flew as soon as they were introduced. Rumours about the nature of their close friendship began to swirl, and the romance was confirmed when they went public for the first time by attending the Screen Actors Guild Awards as a couple at the start of 2011.

While they tried to keep a low profile, the pair found it

hard to hide their true feelings. In one interview Nicholas described Jennifer as 'special' and she in turn happened to mention how good-looking she thought he was, while in another interview he talked about how down to earth he felt Jennifer had stayed, despite her stellar career. He went on to say that dating her meant he had less privacy, but otherwise his life remained unchanged.

Although Jennifer had been linked many times to her *Hunger Games* co-star Josh Hutcherson, and the two friends admitted they did love each other, they insisted they were actually more like 'brother and sister' and there was no romantic connection between them.

Within months of dating, there were suggestions that Nicholas had proposed to Jennifer, but when asked to confirm rumours of an engagement, Jennifer told *Marie Claire* magazine: 'We're so young that it would almost be like if we lived in the same city, what would happen? We'd be living together.

'At least this way he's in the same boat as I am: We can go out and have our own lives and know that we have each other.

'When we're busy, we agree to mutually ignore each other. Not completely, but neither of us gets mad when the other doesn't text back or call. Life's super busy. Obviously you know what they're doing, and you trust them.'

Although they spent much of their relationship apart, due to the demands of hectic filming schedules, the pair managed to enjoy a couple of years together until they appeared to have split up in January 2013.

At the timem a source told *Us Weekly* magazine: 'They just

weren't together a lot, her life is a whirlwind. It just got to be too hard for now.'

Nicholas was then spotted out with Elvis Presley's granddaughter, actress and model Riley Keough, while at a nightclub in New York City, and they appeared to be casually dating until May 2013.

But Jennifer seemed to be taking the split from her first serious boyfriend very much in her stride, and a source revealed that their break-up had been extremely amicable. 'They spent a lot of time apart because of work and it was difficult on their relationship. It was a mutual split. There was no scandal, no cheating,' a close pal of the duo exclusively told *Radar*. 'The distance was just too much. It put a strain on the relationship and it just wasn't working anymore.'

But Riley seemed to be out of the picture when Jennifer and Nicholas were reunited in June 2013. They were thrown back together as they were working alongside one another on the *X-Men* sequel, *Days of Future Past*. To many it appeared as if their brief separation was a distant memory as they were spotted at the cinema together, as well as enjoying romantic lunch dates in their trailers and the two of them even went on a trip to an amusement park during a rare day off.

Jennifer and Nicholas were also seen out and about with their co-stars. They joined James McAvoy, Michael Fassbender and director Bryan Singer at the Canadian Grand Prix, and enjoyed a movie double date with Hugh Jackman and his wife, actress and producer Deborra-Lee Furness.

McAvoy is a huge fan of Jennifer's, and when he picked

up an *Empire* award for Best Sci-Fi Fantasy in March 2015, he joked that she had taken the spotlight from him because of her skimpy costume. 'I'd like to thank Jennifer Lawrence's wonderful blue hue and naked body for ensuring I didn't even feature in that clip,' joked the British actor.

Meanwhile, with their romance very much back on, Jennifer and Nicholas were also spotted at an HBO boxing event, and it seemed that they were delighted to be a couple again.

Jennifer confirmed they were back together in a frank interview with fashion bible *Vogue*, saying: 'He has absolutely no idea how good-looking he is. I think a lot of women and men hate me because of that.' She also joked that they had previously split up over his sloppy attitude to cleaning. 'He would never wring sponges out,' Jennifer explained. 'We were in the kitchen once, and I picked up the sponge, and it was soapy and wet, and I was like, "See? These are the kinds of things that make me think we are never going to work."'

Nevertheless, later that year Nicholas took Jennifer on holiday to Britain to meet his family. His sister Clarista revealed that she was impressed by how down to earth, lovely and easy to talk to Jennifer appeared to be during the visit. 'Jen is lovely. She's really easy to talk to,' she told *Heat* magazine. 'She's really family-orientated, so she fitted in well with us. She doesn't seem like a Hollywood type, she just mucked in.

'We're a very unglam family. In our house, if you want a drink, you get it yourself.'

Jennifer spent some of Christmas 2013 with Nicholas and

his loved ones, but rather than chatting about her upcoming movies or how she had just been nominated for an Oscar for *American Hustle*, the star preferred to be much more low-key. She enjoyed lunch at a local pub and settled down with the Hoult family to watch Christmas television shows. She also apparently helped Nicholas's father Roger make a chicken pie, and baked some cakes.

But reports that the couple were making plans to settle down in Britain by buying a house there together turned out to be false. It was claimed that Jennifer and Nicholas were planning to invest in some property in the English countryside, which they had apparently viewed while visiting over the Christmas holidays.

However, Clarista insisted the pair were a long way from investing in property. Of a home the actor had recently bought in London, she said: 'It's Nick's house, they're not buying it together. It's his first house, he's very excited. He's getting furniture from IKEA.

'They're just a normal couple – they get on really well. They see each other as much as possible and they Skype and FaceTime. She's just really chilled and normal.'

But Clarista suggested that Jennifer might have found Nicholas's family life in Wokingham, Berkshire, a little quiet. She added: 'We don't drink alcohol at home – it's orange squash, that's what she had to be happy with. My mum doesn't drink, so it was how we were brought up. There's no vintage wines or anything like that with dinner. Jen went to the local pub instead for a drink.

'Jen just says what she feels and we're a bit more reserved as a family,' she added.

Nicholas appeared delighted to be by Jennifer's side to support her at the Golden Globes in January 2014, where she picked up the Best Supporting Actress prize for *American Hustle*. He cheered her on at the ceremony, and Jennifer later described how they had played games with a friend's child while getting ready for the show. 'My stylist Rachel [Zoe] brought over her adorable son, Skylar, and we played "tickle monster" for a while,' Jennifer said about her typically chilled-out preparations for the awards. 'I had my friends and family come over, too, so it was like a party, which is always really fun.'

Throughout their relationship there were frequent rumours that the couple were planning to marry, and they emerged publicly again in November 2013 when Jennifer was spotted wearing a new ring on her left hand during a press event for *The Hunger Games: Catching Fire*. And in April 2014 she was seen wearing a turquoise ring while out with Nicholas. She was still wearing it on a trip to London, but later denied any wedding plans, and the couple broke up again in the summer of 2014, once more blaming their hectic schedules. And this time the romance seemed to be over for good, according to reports that the on-again, off-again couple had no choice but to part ways because of the demands of their respective careers.

A source told *E! News*: 'They spent a lot of time apart because of work and it was difficult on their relationship.'

It was not long before Nicholas appeared to have picked

up the pieces and was dating again – he was spotted having lunch with *Twilight* star Kristen Stewart at Daiwa in Tsukiji Fish Market in Los Angeles, and a source explained: 'Nick has been dating several girls for the past few weeks. But he and Jennifer have been broken up longer than people realise.'

According to the *Daily Star*, he and Kristen met while filming their new science fiction movie *Equals* in Japan, just as his relationship with Jennifer was crumbling. Although they had always kept typically tight-lipped about any suggestion of romance, a source told the newspaper that behind closed doors, the new relationship was official: 'Nick is besotted with Kristen. They're a match made in heaven, as they're both anti-fame and share a very strong work ethic.

'Almost as soon as Jennifer told Nick it was over between them, he began seeing Kristen. But they were both worried about making the news public. For one thing, they're private at the best of times, but they also didn't want people thinking there was any overlap in their relationships.'

Kristen and Nicholas spent a great deal of quality time together, both on and off the set. 'Kristen and Nicholas have really connected with each other on so many levels,' an insider told *HollywoodLife.com*. 'They really get each other [with] their wacky sense of humour. They both basically bonded over pranks and pachinko — a really fun kind of arcade game in Japan.

'He brings out her silly self and they just spend a lot of time laughing together and pulling pranks on the cast and crew members. They've become super-tight and it's been healing for both of them to have someone to really lean on,' the source added.

Since all the stars involved are notoriously private, few details were ever confirmed. Some sources say that Nicholas's heart was broken by Jennifer, and his romance with Kristen was little more than a rebound fling. *Celeb Dirty Laundry* suggested Kristen hated Jennifer for that reason, and *Life & Style* claimed that Nicholas was still in love with Jennifer. An insider reportedly told the magazine that Jennifer was still the love of his life, and they would be getting back together, making any new relationship impossible.

It also emerged that Kristen was only dating Nicholas to get back at her former boyfriend and *Twilight* co-star Robert Pattinson, who had also moved on and was now in a relationship with British singer-songwriter FKA Twigs, better known as Tahliah Barnett.

While Jennifer was not short of men wanting to date her, and friends said she was not in a hurry to jump into another relationship because she was too busy with work, it was only a matter of weeks before she was first linked to Coldplay frontman Chris Martin.

The initial suggestion of romance between them sparked headlines across the globe since the British musician had recently split from his wife, Hollywood superstar Gwyneth Paltrow.

Shortly before the rumours began to swirl, Jennifer said in an interview that she was ready to date again. 'Basically, what I'm saying is all I need in a relationship is somebody to watch TV with me,' she said, before adding that she also wants a guy who will be super comfortable around her and feel like he can be himself – in every way: 'You know, a guy who isn't afraid to fart in front of me,' she said. 'Also, rather than have big, passionate love I'd rather have just a peaceful time. Those relationships are deeper because you can be your true self with somebody, and somebody can be their true self with you.

'I don't like fighting, and I find argumentative people the most annoying people on the planet. Like, why do you still want to be fighting? It's just unattractive. I would just rather have somebody that has the same taste in reality TV,' she told *Vanity Fair*.

And when asked about her budding romance with Martin by French magazine *Madame Figaro*, Jennifer appeared very embarrassed, as they had only been dating a matter of weeks. She giggled and stammered: 'I do seem to like Englishmen, don't I? Oh gosh, I don't know. You guys [Englishmen] are just so charming. Oh God, now I'm blushing and scratching and itching and sweating.'

While there were suggestions that Jennifer had perhaps started dating Chris before he and Gwyneth officially ended their ten-year marriage, this was never confirmed. The pair were first officially linked three months after his much-publicised 'conscious uncoupling' from Gwyneth. The high-profile power-couple announced their somewhat unconventional split on Gwyneth's lifestyle website *Goop*, which has often been mocked for advocating unusual diets, expensive designer clothing and wacky beauty fads, such as vaginal steaming!

In a blog post revealing the end of their marriage, Gwyneth wrote: 'It is with hearts full of sadness that we have decided to separate.

'We are parents first and foremost, to two incredibly wonderful children, and we ask for their space and privacy to be respected at this difficult time. We have always conducted our relationship privately, and we hope that as we consciously uncouple and co-parent, we will be able to continue in the same manner.'

But the carefully chosen wording of their announcement caused much amusement and mockery – especially on Twitter. British publicist Mark Borkowski identified 'conscious uncoupling' as the phrase of the morning, and at the end of the day blogger Perez Hilton signed off with: 'I'm going to consciously uncouple from my laptop now. I kindly ask for privacy while I sleep.'

Businesses 'consciously uncoupled' from their directors, and actor Colin Firth announced his 'conscious uncoupling' from the voice of Paddington Bear when Ben Whishaw took over the role. Meanwhile the Plain English Foundation declared the phrase to be 2014's worst example of spin and jargon.

Months later, Gwyneth admitted that the phrase was 'kind of goofy', but added that it simply boiled down to separation 'with minimal acrimony'.

She said: 'We've made a lot of mistakes, and we've had good days and bad days but I have to say, I'm proud of us for working through so much stuff together and not naming and shaming.'

In April 2014, Chris told BBC Radio 1's Zane Lowe that he felt he had to split from Gwyneth in order to work on his own emotional wellbeing. 'I wouldn't use the word breakdown,' he said, when asked about the end of his marriage. 'This was more a realisation about trying to grow up, basically. If you can't open yourself up, you can't appreciate the wonder inside. So you can be with someone very wonderful, but because of your own issues you cannot let that be celebrated in the right way.'

He went on to tell the DJ: 'What changed for me was, I don't want to go through life being scared of it, being scared of love, being scared of rejection, being scared of failure.

'About two years ago I was a mess really because I can't enjoy the thing that we are good at, and I can't enjoy the great things around me because I'm burdened by this. I've got to not blame anyone else and make some changes.'

While Chris seemed to move seamlessly on to his low-key romance with Jennifer pretty swiftly, many sources say they had in fact agreed to take their relationship very slowly for the sake of his two children, Apple and Moses.

It later emerged that he and Gwyneth had quietly separated about a year before making the actual announcement – which came as a shock because two months prior to their official split, they made the usual move of appearing in public together three times. Although they had gone to great lengths throughout their marriage to avoid being photographed together, the pair made a rare show of togetherness over the Golden Globes weekend in 2014, culminating in Gwyneth singing his praises at the awards bash held at the Beverly Hilton Hotel.

While *Iron Man* actress Gwyneth was not up for an award that year, Chris was nominated for Best Original Song from the soundtrack to *The Hunger Games: Catching Fire*, with a song called 'Atlas' by his band Coldplay. Few could have predicted that in a matter of months, in an unexpected turn of events, the couple would be estranged and Chris would be dating *The Hunger Games'* leading lady.

In July 2014, during an interview with the *Valentine in the Morning* radio show, Chris confirmed he was back on the market, and once again opened up about his relationship with Gwyneth post-split, saying: 'The thing we told everyone at the beginning of the year is true. We are very close. We are not together. But we're, you know, that's the truth and that's it. You know, there's a lot of love. No scandal, I'm afraid. I wish I could give you scandal.'

Jennifer, meanwhile, made it clear she was also available, and looking for her ideal man, just as her romance with Chris gradually began to gather momentum. The couple were spotted together on several different occasions, despite their best efforts to keep a low profile in the early stages.

A source told *People* magazine: 'Even though they are busy, the relationship is solid. They see each other when they can. Jennifer understands that the children come first with Chris and that his relationship with Gwyneth is based around the family and will always be a part of his life. Things are good between them.'

However, the cat was well and truly out of the bag in the summer of 2014 when Jennifer was spotted kissing Chris at a Kings of Leon concert in LA. Up until that point they had managed to keep their romance under wraps, rarely being pictured in the same place at the same time. But it had proved impossible for the relationship to go on undetected any longer.

Sparks had first flown after they had been introduced following a Coldplay concert at the Royal Albert Hall: 'Jen was blown away at his London show. His music is absolutely part of the attraction,' a source told *Us Weekly*. 'The better she gets to know him, the more she likes him.'

It seemed they had hit it off immediately when first introduced at the after-party held at the Kensington Roof Gardens in London, following the concert.

After texting for six weeks and enjoying a few initial dates, Chris introduced Jennifer to his friends over dinner and then to his grandparents. She in turn took him to meet her parents. But they kept it quiet until the Kings of Leon concert at the Hollywood Bowl, where Chris was a surprise performer. Jennifer was spotted taking pictures of him on her phone while he played piano on two numbers. After the concert, it was reported on gossip website *Just Jared*: 'They engaged playfully with each other, appearing like a couple in love. She kissed him on the lips several times.'

Us Weekly reported that Jennifer had arrived with friends and Chris seemed to be looking for her, then when he performed on stage he could not take his eyes off his new girlfriend. 'Just before the show was supposed to start, Jennifer Lawrence walked toward the stage, surrounded by a couple girlfriends, trying to find their seat,' a source said. 'They looked a little rushed, like they wanted to get to their seat before the show started, so someone on the theatre staff helped them out.'

The insider continued: 'Chris gave a good look around the room and then spotted someone up on the balcony. He pointed and said, "Aha! I see you!" and then smiled and waved. He kept looking up in the direction during the show and smiling, pointing, singing to her.'

A source told *E! News* that Jennifer 'danced the entire time and knew every word to every song.'

The insider continued: 'She couldn't take her eyes off him. Jennifer stared adoringly at Chris, both hands in the air, dancing and singing along to "Magic".'

After the show she left through a back exit, trying to leave unnoticed by holding her handbag over her face as she was led towards a waiting car.

That was the first official contact between the two, although Jennifer had been spotted at a number of Chris's gigs in various locations over the previous three months, and spectators had started to suggest that she was rather more than just another devoted fan. Shortly after that now infamous Kings of Leon gig, she was seen backstage, taking pictures of Chris as he performed at the sell-out *iHeartRadio* Music Festival in Las Vegas.

Jennifer was pictured walking around backstage at the festival, where Chris and his band were performing. While the pair had yet to confirm their romance the official Twitter account of *iHeartRadio* hinted that they were already going strong: 'SPOTTED #JenniferLawrence Backstage! Wonder who she's here to see? ★Cough New b/f #ChrisMartin Cough★ #iHeartRadio,' a post read.

And a source told *RadarOnline.com*: 'At around 7pm on Friday night, Jennifer and Chris were making out backstage in an area that only allows security and a select group of celebrities in.

'She had her arms around his neck. They were kissing passionately before he took the stage!

'Jennifer was watching from backstage and looked like the proudest girlfriend in the world! They spent the entire weekend together. They were not trying to hide it at all.'

After two songs had played – 'Talihina Sky' and 'Notion' – the pair were snapped together making their return to Los Angeles by private jet, and by that stage things were clearly getting serious. Just a few weeks later they were spotted on a romantic dinner date at La Dolce Vita in Beverly Hills, according to *People* magazine: 'They were super cute together,' an eyewitness said. 'They were laughing a lot and Jennifer was acting all goofy!'

And a source told *HollywoodLife.com*: 'The evening took a romantic turn when Jennifer leaned over the table to get a kiss and was met halfway by a waiting Chris. That really was the most PDA [Public Display of Affection] that was seen during the dinner, but they definitely were having a blast. Plus, the way the seats are, they are more like a booth feel, so they were next to each other and close.'

The site also reported that the couple shared a bottle of red wine and also their food: 'They had a lot of food, calamari, a couple of pastas, the steak, I don't remember everything they had but I was impressed because they ordered a lot and they finished it all,' the source added.

And although they had not been dating very long at that stage, Chris was supportive of Jennifer when the hacking scandal broke, and nude photos of her were leaked on to the internet; he himself had years of experience when it came to handling public scrutiny.

'Chris has been right there for Jen. She doesn't know how she would have got through this without him,' an insider told *Grazia* magazine. 'Chris is being totally calm and like a rock. He has deep feelings for Jennifer and is broken-hearted that she's been targeted in such an intrusive way.'

After the initial shots were posted on a photo-sharing website, it was claimed Jennifer had sought refuge at Chris's Malibu home. He was not staying there at the time as he was spending time with Gwyneth and their children, but let her use his house to escape the press attention.

He had apparently tried to reassure her, saying the situation would run out of steam, but when that showed no sign of happening and a second wave of photos was released shortly after, Chris made sure Jennifer had all the practical and emotional help she needed.

'Jennifer is one of the hottest actresses in Hollywood, so of course she is worried about what people think. She also feels violated and betrayed. Privately, she tried to laugh it off the first time, but to have it happen a second time is horrific,' a source explained.

Another source added that Chris and Jennifer had fallen for each other and despite the embarrassment caused by the scandal, he had no plans to leave her: 'Chris doesn't care that Jennifer took naked pics of herself, he's more concerned that her privacy was invaded,' a source told *HollywoodLife. com.* 'The whole thing is disturbing and Chris has just been very supportive.'

The source revealed that Chris is not the kind of man who would break up with Jennifer when she needed him most: 'He would never end things with Jennifer over something like this. The couple are using humour to get through this negative situation. It will pass, that's what he tells her. And he just uses his quirky sense of humour to help her look at the funny side. They both do a lot of laughing together, which is what really attracted them to each other in the first place.

'Jen is horrified over this leak and knows that this will possibly affect her upcoming roles.

'She knows that A-list stars don't have this type of controversy attached to them and is very much horrified over the whole situation.'

Chris apparently told friends that he was attracted to Jennifer because she was the polar opposite of Gwyneth: 'Jennifer is loads of fun and they can't stop laughing when they are together,' a source told *The Sun* newspaper. 'Chris feels he is dating someone who has everything he's been missing out on in the past eleven years.'

Friends believed that Jennifer was a good boost for Chris following his split from clean-living Gwyneth, who is renowned for her healthy diet and strict fitness routine, while Jennifer smokes and drinks, loves red meat, only exercises when she has to and admits she enjoys tucking into junk food.

The source added that Chris felt the *Hunger Games* star had given him a 'new lease of life', adding, 'Jennifer doesn't take herself too seriously and when she is not filming she just wants to hang out and have a good time.'

And their budding relationship took a serious turn when the Coldplay singer started to write love songs about his new girlfriend: 'He writes her songs and loves taking her to private romantic spots. Chris is sweeping Jen off her feet. That's his thing,' an insider told *Us Weekly*.

They also shared a special afternoon together at the Wölffer Estate Vineyard in California to celebrate Jennifer's twenty-fourth birthday in August 2014: 'They were there on a date,' the source dished. 'They were very low-key, nobody realised who they were. The setting was super-romantic. They watched the sun go down.'

But their initial happiness was plagued by suggestions that Gwyneth was still very much on the scene, with some saying that she and Chris were actually involved in an open relationship, and were even considering a surprise reunion.

That said, reports were certainly confused and conflicted, as *E! News* reported: 'On weekends, if one of them has the kids and the other doesn't have plans, Chris Martin and Gwyneth Paltrow will meet up and do something all together. They truly love one another and think the world of each other, they just aren't a couple.

'They will spend the holidays together and make sure the kids know they are always going to be a family.'

Another problem widely speculated upon was the thirteen-year age gap between Chris and Jennifer, and by October 2014 they appeared to have cooled things off as Chris spent Thanksgiving, Christmas and what would have been his eleventh wedding anniversary with Gwyneth, Apple and Moses. And at that time it began to look as if Jennifer would be left out in the cold as reports suggested that Chris was reuniting with his ex-wife.

He was a surprise performer at the amfAR gala in Los Angeles in October 2014, and Gwyneth, who hosted the event, was by his side all night. She kicked off the event by bringing Chris and his bandmate Jonny Buckland up on stage to perform the band's hit songs, 'Paradise' and 'Viva La Vida'. Introducing them, she gushed openly about her former husband, whom she described as Father of the Year to the crowd. 'This brilliant singer-songwriter has sold 8 million records,' said Gwyneth. 'He has won every single award that there is to be won, especially Father of the Year, which he has won consecutively since 2004.

'I am speaking of Chris Martin,' she added, 'and the incredibly talented Jonny Buckland, who together make up one-half of the legendary band Coldplay.'

There was still no suggestion that Chris had been in touch with Jennifer to offer her any words of reassurance when he was spotted with Gwyneth shortly after the gala at a sushi restaurant in Los Angeles, where his estranged wife was seen tenderly stroking his face. There were even suggestions that Gwyneth herself had called the paparazzi to capture the intimate moment in an attempt to drive a wedge between Chris and Jennifer.

And that same night, a glum-looking Jennifer was pictured elsewhere in the city having dinner with a friend, apparently furious that Chris and Gwyneth still appeared so close.

But then Gwyneth decided to go public with her new boyfriend, *Glee* producer Brad Falchuk, who she took to the premiere of her new film, *Mortdecai*. Not only did she hold hands with him, but she also made sure that photographers captured every romantic moment between them.

The situation confused Jennifer and as she struggled to make sense of it all, she escaped to the solace of her family home. A source told *MailOnline*: 'Jen got tired of watching Chris play happy families with Gwyn and was annoyed that he was trying to keep her hidden away.'

While Chris was spotted in Malibu having dinner and celebrating the holidays with Gwyneth in an apparent attempt to keep the season as normal as possible for their young children, Jennifer flew home to Kentucky to spend the Thanksgiving holidays with her family in 2014.

She cheered herself up by rooting for the Louisville Cardinals, her hometown college basketball team, standing out among a crowd of revellers, cheering and flashing signals as the NCAA college basketball game got underway. As images of her were beamed onto the scoreboard, prompting cheers from the crowd, the actress formed an 'L'-shape with her hand as a sign of support for her favourite team, who were playing against the Kentucky Wildcats.

She even wore a black University of Louisville T-shirt, skinny jeans and a red Louisville Cardinals cap during the game at the KFC Yum! Center. Her team lost by eight points, but in a video posted to YouTube, she could be seen performing the university's 'C-A-R-D-S' cheer and enjoying a slice of pizza.

Before the start of the game she'd been ushered to the locker room, where she posed for a photo with radio personality Terry Meiners.

For her part, Jennifer was certainly doing her best not to be seen to be pining for her boyfriend; instead she tried to make the most of a normal holiday with her family. Renowned for her down-to-earth approach to fame, she followed a traditional turkey dinner with a day spent shopping with pals. And practical Jennifer dressed for some serious bargain hunting at the holiday sales in comfy flats, jeans and a long cardigan jacket. Her skin was make-up free and a simple beanie covered her hair.

But there were suggestions that Chris could be back in touch, as Jennifer seemed to be spending an awful lot of time checking her phone. As she joined the scrum of Black Friday shoppers hunting down bargains, it appeared she was taking a call from her on-off lover. Whoever was on the line, Jennifer was certainly very happy to hear from the caller, grinning as she saw their name on the screen.

Whether or not he was checking in by phone, Chris's absence came as a major disappointment for Jennifer's grandmother, who had been very excited about meeting him. Carolyn Koch told the *Sun On Sunday* that she was expecting him to join in the family's celebrations: 'Jennifer's mum flew to Los Angeles to meet Chris,' she explained of her daughter Karen. 'We will have to get another chair for the dinner table at Christmas. The family is getting so big we might have to split up for gatherings.'

Although neither Jennifer nor Chris was prepared to discuss any aspect of their relationship, they did manage to meet up whenever their schedules would allow.

Meanwhile, Gwyneth had first met TV producer Brad Falchuk in 2010 when she guest-starred on the hit musical-comedy drama series *Glee* as a glamorous Spanish teacher. In March 2013, his marriage to wife Suzanne, with whom he has two children, ended in divorce and there were even whispers that an affair with Gwyneth was the reason behind it.

In August 2014, Gwyneth and Brad spent a romantic weekend at the luxurious Amangiri luxury resort in Utah, with an eyewitness telling American magazine *Star*: 'They were lying next to each other, Gwyneth was topless.'

Their relationship dipped below the radar after that sighting, when it appeared that Gwyneth and Chris could be heading for a reunion, but then in January 2015 she was holding hands with Brad at a party following the premiere of her new film, *Mordecai*, in LA: 'Their relationship has been stop-start, but is finally getting off the ground,' a source told *Grazia* magazine.

'After finally agreeing to dissolve her relationship with Chris, Gwyneth is ready to take things to the next level with Brad. Bringing him as her date to Robert's birthday was a big step.'

And so, having been patient for well over a year, Jennifer and Brad seemed to finally be getting the romances they had waited for: 'Both Brad and Jen have previously expressed dismay at being third wheels in Chris and Gwyneth's marriage,' the source explained to *Grazia*. 'Eventually, they both realised that they couldn't keep living in limbo, and would have to make the final cut in order to move on with their lives.'

But while she waited for Chris to extricate himself from his complex marital situation, Jennifer was forced to deny that she was romantically involved with her close friend Bradley Cooper. Speculation had always been rife that the close-knit pair were more than just good friends and they were spotted leaving a New York hotel together in March 2015.

At a party following a gala screening of their film *Serena*, Jennifer told *Us Weekly* magazine: 'We are pretty much work husband and wife, you could say. But there is no sex! I know what you're thinking!'

But the next day Bradley left a hotel in Tribeca with Jennifer, carrying her dog Pippa under his arm. The intimate gesture caused many to speculate that there was more to their friendship than met their eye, and they were branded 'The new Brad and Jen' in reference to one of Hollywood's most infamous A-list couplings, between Brad Pitt and Jennifer Aniston.

Grazia magazine reported that Bradley's on-off girlfriend, British model and actress Suki Waterhouse, was unhappy when she saw the pictures, adding that Jennifer and Bradley were being seen as a hot new couple. 'They've always shared a great vibe – they hit it off straight away when they first began filming together and have been close ever since,' a source told the magazine. 'They genuinely enjoy each other's company.

'The timing hasn't been right before, but it's different now and friends think it's only a matter of time before they hook up. Bradley has been leaning on Jen since splitting from Suki and they've become even closer. There's always been chemistry between them – even if they won't admit it, everyone else can see it.'

But just as the rumours began to gather pace, Bradley was spotted hugging Suki at the Coachella music festival in April. The pair hung out with veteran actor Clint Eastwood at the event in California, and there was no sign of Jennifer, who spent Easter Sunday with Chris – he flew into Boston where she was filming on a private jet from New Jersey.

Just as she dismissed suggestions that she was dating Bradley, Jennifer was also dealing with hints that romance was blossoming with her *Hunger Games* co-star Liam Hemsworth, who had endured a high-profile split from singer Miley Cyrus roughly a year earlier.

According to a report in *Heat* magazine: 'They've always had insane chemistry, but they've never been single at the same time before. In fact, when they first met on the set of *The Hunger Games*, Liam's then-fiancée Miley Cyrus flew out, possibly to keep an eye on them, I think, because she was jealous.'

It seemed the *Wrecking Ball* star was planning to talk to Jennifer at a Christmas party at the end of 2014. 'Miley wants a showdown,' an insider said. 'She's told everyone she's planning to confront Jen at [Australian TV presenter] Paul Khoury's party in a few weeks – he's Liam's best friend and he stayed friends with Miley after the split.

'Paul knows Jen through Liam, so all of them are invited. Jen has no idea what's coming. She hates confrontation, but it would be a chance to settle the score. Liam would be furious and, if he finds out, he may try to stop Miley going. Miley always suspected Jen is the real reason Liam wouldn't get back with her,' the source added.

Liam and Miley started dating in 2009, when they co-starred in the Nicholas Sparks' film, *The Last Song*. In 2012, Liam proposed with a 3.5-carat Neil Lane diamond ring, but the couple made their last public appearance together at the premiere of his film *Paranoia* at the DGA Theater Complex in Los Angeles, before he officially announced his split from her at the end of 2013.

'Jen and Liam have been friends for years and she's always confided in him about the drama in her love life. She's really leaned on him during all the drama with Chris Martin,' the *Heat* report continued. 'Jen started pouring her heart out about Chris and things got personal. Liam knows Jen loves koala bears so, the next day, he had an enormous stuffed toy koala sent to Jen with a note saying, "Hold out for the perfect man".'

Jennifer had raved about her handsome Australian co-star

in an interview with *Nylon* magazine, saying: 'I guess the thing that surprised me is that I would never expect to ever have a man this good-looking ever be my best friend.

'I just would never assume those things could happen, but he is. He's the most wonderful, lovable, family-oriented, sweet, hilarious, amazing guy.'

She went on to credit the younger brother of Australian actors Chris and Luke Hemsworth for teaching her to stand up for herself: 'It's my biggest weakness: negotiating. I'm a wimp about standing up for myself and Liam is always fair. He's always on time, he's always doing his job, and he's good about making sure that things stay fair. He's teaching me to toughen up a little bit. That was important, I need that.'

And it seemed that Liam felt exactly the same way about Jennifer: 'You couldn't ask for a better co-star than her, she's great,' the 6ft 3in heart-throb said of the actress on *Good Morning America*. 'Jennifer cares about the people around her, she has a big heart, she's amazing at it,' Liam told Robin Roberts.

Although there was nothing to suggest an actual romance had begun Liam had reportedly been single since a very brief fling with actress Eiza González earlier that year. But he still managed to crack a joke about having to film romantic scenes with Jennifer: 'Any time I had to kiss Jennifer was pretty uncomfortable,' the actor told chat show host Jimmy Fallon. 'When you look at it on the outside it looks like a great picture. She's one of my best friends. I love her.

'But if we had a kissing scene, she would make a point of eating garlic or tuna fish or something that was disgusting.'

Although Jennifer continued to insist that she and Liam were nothing more than very good friends, in a separate interview with the *Associated Press*, Liam spoke movingly about their friendship, adding that she had helped him deal with the fallout after calling off his wedding to Miley Cyrus. 'For a few years, I went down a path where I forgot to be in the moment and enjoy the moment,' he revealed. 'But being around someone like Jen, who is so honest and laughs all day long, I am forced to be in the moment right now. I'm much happier.'

Naturally, their kind words about each other led to speculation, and *OK!* magazine was among the many media outlets reporting regularly on the suggestion of a budding romance. One source claimed that their romance first began around the time that Jennifer was getting over the nude photo leak, which came at the same time as her relationship with Chris briefly cooled: 'It happened while they were in Germany, promoting the movie, having a heart-to-heart in Liam's hotel room. Jennifer was overwhelmed by all the publicity surrounding her split from Chris Martin and her nude photo scandal, and he was more than happy to listen to her vent,' said the source, who went on to reveal that consolation from Liam brought out romantic feelings in them both.

'Liam said something to lighten the mood, making Jen laugh, then she wrapped her arms around him to give him a hug. Jennifer definitely had a moment. It was as if she suddenly knew he was The One,' the source added.

'Liam obviously felt it too, because they decided then and there that they wanted to be together.'

The source went on to suggest that while there 'has always been a connection', it was not until this specific moment that everything suddenly clicked into place.

According to *OK!* magazine Jennifer and Liam had a sudden moment of realisation that they were indeed secret soul mates. Another insider claimed that 'Jennifer definitely had a moment' with Liam.

And according to *Heat* magazine: 'They intend on keeping things very low-key so they can both see where fate takes them. They've always had insane chemistry, but they've never been single at the same time before. Jen and Liam have been friends for years, and she's always confided in him about the drama in her love life. She's really leaned on him during all the drama with Chris.'

The pair had also apparently bonded over their love of dogs – Liam is known as a 'dog whisperer' among the *Hunger Games* cast. The actor, who stars as Gale Hawthorne in the film franchise, is always especially happy to share his pet wisdom: 'Liam always gives me dog advice. Which I don't actually ask for. He's what I call a pet supremist,' Jennifer laughed to *Heat* magazine.

Liam interjected: 'Well, if your dog's gonna be an idiot and piss everywhere and you're not gonna know what to do with it…'

'He's a whisperer, a dog whisperer,' co-star Josh Hutcherson added.

Jennifer agreed that Liam is good at training wayward hounds, but she refuses to listen to his pet tips, as her pooch is too 'cute' to reprimand.

The tight-knit trio was also quizzed on whether their friendship means they now do kind things for each other. Initially they insisted they do not, before the Jennifer admitted she does have a sweeter side.

'I did get Josh a helicopter drone for his birthday,' she explained. 'I was worried he'd guess what it was, so I told him it was one of those remote control vacuum cleaners you control with your phone, and he believed me. So I was like, "I'm just kidding – it's a helicopter!" But Liam and I don't really do anything nice.'

That might not be strictly true, as Jennifer and Liam appeared to be closer than ever on the publicity trail. Their flirtatious behaviour certainly seemed to suggest that they were in the early stages of a romance, and by the end of their promotional tour Jennifer was sad to be parting ways: 'I think we're done with the press tour. I've got, like, one more thing to shoot for *Hunger Games*. We just have one scene to do for the end,' she told *Interview* magazine. 'I'm not happy about it at all. And now Liam's doing a movie in Australia for two months. It's the longest that the three of us have ever spent apart.'

It was also reported that Jennifer's family were pushing for her to take her relationship with Liam to the next level: 'Liam and Jen have always been close – there's a real bond between them and they turn to each other when they have problems,' an insider told *Heat*. 'Her friends and family are desperate for her to ditch Chris – they feel Liam's a better match and doesn't carry all the baggage of Gwyneth and children.

'It has been difficult for Jennifer to get her head around, which is why she has been leaning on Liam.

'Jen wants commitment from Chris, but he is still spending time with Gwyneth because of the kids. Jen's sometimes lonely and Liam is filling that gap. They're in contact all the time. There's genuine love there between them,' the insider added.

Other friends of Jennifer reportedly hoped she would finish with Chris and end up with Liam.

'There's definitely some kind of "race" on between Chris and Gwyneth to see who can settle down first with a new partner,' *OK!* magazine reported.

Heat revisited the idea that she might end up with Liam: "Liam and Jen have always been close – there's a real bond between them and they turn to each other when they have problems," a source told the magazine. "Her friends and family are desperate for her to ditch Chris – they feel Liam's a better match and doesn't carry all the baggage of Gwyneth and children."

Other sources suggested that Chris and Jennifer had cooled their romance after just four months of dating because he felt insecure about her hunky bodyguard. Indeed Justin Riblet had caused quite a sensation when he was photographed escorting the actress through Los Angeles International Airport in December 2014, sparking a Twitter frenzy. Chris was supposedly none too happy with all the attention. *Celeb*

Dirty Laundry reported that Chris feared there was 'more to their relationship than just security details'.

The fact that Riblet is well-rounded and educated, as well as handsome, only increased Chris's anxiety, and many fans openly wondered why Jennifer would date Chris when she was with Riblet round the clock.

'He looks like a freaking model,' one Twitter user wrote.

'If I were Jennifer, that would be my next boyfriend,' another fan wrote. 'I want to be Jennifer for one day with JR by my side.'

Meanwhile *The Cut* magazine branded him 'The Hottyguard'.

According to Riblet's LinkedIn profile, he is a graduate of Rutgers University and holds a degree in Criminal Justice. He graduated in 2007 and spent five years with the US Army, serving as a Special Forces weapons sergeant.

While there was no evidence to suggest he and Jennifer enjoyed anything beyond a professional relationship, she would not of course be the first celebrity to have fallen for their bodyguard. Supermodel Heidi Klum was romantically involved with her bodyguard Martin Kirsten for about eighteen months before they called it quits following the break-up of her marriage to the British musician Seal. Other celebrities who reportedly fell for their bodyguards include Amy Winehouse, Britney Spears, Kate Gosselin, Scarlett Johansson and Kim Kardashian. And Karl Lagerfeld's bodyguard, Sebastien Jondeau, is so attractive the creative director of Chanel chose him to star in advertising campaigns.

Around the same time as her cooling-off period from Chris Martin, Jennifer had to deal with yet more dating rumours after she was spotted hanging out at movie producer Gabe Polsky's house for more than five hours one evening. 'They ordered a couple of pizzas and about 30 minutes later another delivery man came with more pizza,' a source told the *New York Daily News*. 'They definitely weren't in there reading scripts. They were having a good time.'

She was seen arriving at the Beverly Hills home of the handsome film producer and director with her little dog Pippi in her arms, dressed down in workout gear. Jennifer sported a grey hoodie and leggings, along with trainers and a black tank top and wore a white beanie over her blonde hair.

She had a brief scare when her pup ran out on the street, but Polsky came to the rescue and retrieved her pet. A source told the *Daily News* website: 'The two were spotted hanging out at his residence for about five hours, with Lawrence departing later that night. During their time together, the duo ordered pizza – not once, but twice.'

Although he had been dating one of Jennifer's best friends and the pair could have been discussing work on a future project together, there were immediate suggestions that there was more to her friendship with Gabe Polsky – who just so happens to bear quite a resemblance to one Chris Martin.

Polsky wrote, directed and produced *Red Army* (2014), a documentary about the Soviet Union and its ice hockey team. With his brother Alan he owns production company Polsky Films, the studio behind Nicolas Cage's *Bad Lieutenant: Port Of*

Call New Orleans (2009). The brothers have also collaborated on other movies, including *The Motel Life* (2013), which starred Emile Hirsch, Stephen Dorff, Kris Kristofferson and Dakota Fanning, and *Little Birds* (2011), starring Juno Temple, Kate Bosworth and Leslie Mann.

The scrutiny proved overwhelming for Jennifer, and on Christmas Eve 2014 she fled Hollywood again and flew back home to be with her family. During her brief trip to Kentucky she found the time to pose for photos with children at Louisville's Kosair Children's Hospital. Jennifer delighted dozens of families of sick children with bedside visits, including Gage Besing, a six-year-old boy battling Diffuse Intrinsic Pontine Glioma.

Jennifer also visited Tyler Foster from Muhlenberg County, who was being treated for bone cancer. Tyler's family posted on Facebook that the one celebrity he wanted to meet was Jennifer Lawrence – and his wish came true.

While Jennifer was away, Chris enjoyed the festivities with his family. 'It wasn't dramatic,' an insider told *E! News*. 'Things just didn't work out,' the source continued, adding Chris and Jennifer had split a few weeks before the news went public. 'There are no hard feelings between them.'

Whether he and Jennifer had parted ways or not, Chris appeared to be very much with his ex-wife and kids when Christmas rolled around. He and Gwyneth took their children to Tribeca's i-Plaza Nail & Spa: 'They seemed very affectionate toward each other,' a source told *PageSix*.

The estranged couple were 'laughing a lot, making jokes,

and Chris even had his arm around Gwyneth,' said another source. Chris also entertained his children by dancing and singing along to Christmas carols playing in the salon, while he waited for Apple to finish her manicure.

Apparently Gwyneth had hated the idea of her first Christmas as a single woman and she did not want Apple and Moses to have to split their time between their parents. An insider told *Closer* magazine: 'She suggested he come over for the holidays. She's asked him to invite his family, too, and she's planning a big Christmas Eve party and massive feast the next day.

'Gwyneth said last year's festivities were so tense between her and Chris, but now they're in a much better place and they can really enjoy themselves,' the source added.

And days later they seemed 'inseparable' during the opening of a Goop store in Dallas, which of course had nothing to do with the children. 'They tried to avoid the cameras, but he stuck to her like glue. There was a tenderness that you'd associate with a couple in love,' a source told *Radar Online*.

They also travelled to New York together to support their mutual friend Cameron Diaz when she hosted *Saturday Night Live*. 'Despite being separated, they've been awfully affectionate! There's a buzz among their friends that they are still sleeping together,' a source said. 'They even stayed in the same hotel rooms in both Texas and New York.'

Neither Gwyneth nor Chris made any suggestion that they might consider reconciliation, but their closeness was believed to be the reason Jennifer kept her distance over the holidays. She was said to have often felt like a third wheel when she was with Chris, and felt like she had no choice but to step back while he remained so close to his ex. According to a *HollywoodLife* source: 'Jennifer just couldn't compete and didn't want to. Chris is clearly not over Gwyneth and his main priority is his kids. Jennifer really respects him, but she wants a man of her own. And Chris has been spending lots of time with Gwyneth and their kids lately.

'It was just a bit too much for Jen. She doesn't want to be second to anyone. You can't blame her. Gwyneth still has a lot of control over him, which isn't exactly desirable to prospective girlfriends.

'The way things are at the moment, no sane person would want to be an accessory to their conscious uncoupling.'

It then emerged that Chris was planning to take time off from his band to focus on his personal life, and fans expressed their shock when it was suggested that Jennifer had threatened to walk away for good unless he stopped spending all his free time with Gwyneth.

'It's hard for her to understand the feelings between Chris and Gwyneth,' a source told *Celeb Dirty Laundry*: 'It's unclear whether Jennifer dumped Chris because she figured out he was still sleeping with Gwyneth, or if Chris and Jennifer had a completely unrelated falling out, so he ran and hopped back in bed with Gwyneth because he can't stand to be single for a day.

'Regardless of the circumstance, one thing is for sure, Chris Martin is playing a dangerous game.'

At the end of December 2014, Gwyneth confessed that she still sometimes had doubts about splitting from Chris. The actress spoke candidly to *Harper's Bazaar* magazine and explained that there are times when she thinks it would be better if they had stayed married: 'We've made a lot of mistakes, and we've had good days and bad days, but, I have to say, I'm proud of us for working through so much stuff together – and not blaming and shaming.

'Of course, there are times when I think it would have been better if we had stayed married, which is always what your children want. But we have been able to solidify this friendship, so that we're really close.'

The family had relocated from London to Los Angeles, and Gwyneth revealed how happy she felt following the move. 'There's a deep comfort about it because it's so familiar. The other day I was lying on the grass and the kids were playing and I was looking at the sky and the palm-trees – and there was something about the weather and the smell and I was, like, eight years old again,' she said. 'I had such a strong memory of being a kid here. It's a really nice place to be a little kid, and it's great to watch my children have that experience.'

But as soon as the Christmas holidays were behind them, Jennifer and Chris reunited and appeared to be doing their best to get back on track again.

They saw in the New Year together – to everyone's surprise they were spotted at a Japanese restaurant in LA, leading to fevered speculation that they had rekindled their low-key romance. A photo emerged of the pair sitting in a quiet restaurant called Kiwami Sushi in the Studio City area, chatting happily across the table as they ate with chopsticks.

Jennifer wore a grey jacket and black trousers, while Chris was equally casual, sporting a thick layer of facial stubble. Despite suggestions that Jennifer had ended the relationship because she felt Gwyneth's meddling had became too much for her to handle, they both appeared happier than ever.

An eyewitness said: 'They were engulfed in their little world of conversation. They were into each other and not noticing anyone else around them. They seemed to be just content with each other. He was really listening to what she was saying.'

And from then on, things became better than ever for the couple, with Jennifer even planning a style and fashion makeover. Friends revealed that while she is known for her modest and classy wardrobe, Jennifer wanted to update her image to fit into the live music scene: 'She really wants to look cool as the girlfriend of a rock god,' an insider told the American edition of *OK!* magazine. 'This new relationship will see her immersed in a whole new lifestyle involving concerts and tours. She's totally into the whole scene and loving her new life as the leading lady of a music legend.'

According to the whispers, Jennifer was eager to get rid of her 'gawky image' and replace it with something more alternative: 'She has splashed out on a whole range of new edgy T-shirts and jeans so she looks the part backstage when Chris is performing.

'It's all part of her "I don't care" approach to life since the humiliation of her nude picture leaks,' the source concluded.

Chris and Jennifer decided to make their romance official when they made a public appearance together after both being invited to celebrate Harry Styles's twenty-first birthday at a glitzy star-studded bash in February 2015. As well as the One Direction star's Victoria's Secret model girlfriend Nadine Leopold, other guests at the raucous party at Lulu's Cafe in LA included David Beckham, Adele, Courtney Cox and Cara Delevingne.

It was the first time the couple had openly attended such a high-profile event together, and according to website *Just Jared*, they stuck by each other's side throughout the £200,000 bash. But apparently their display left British model Alexa Chung feeling 'totally thrown' since she and Chris had briefly enjoyed a few dates following his split from Gwyneth but their relationship had never really got off the ground: 'Alexa hadn't seen Chris since they dated last year and was totally thrown when he walked in holding hands with Jennifer Lawrence,' a source told *Closer*. 'She avoided them all night and got a little upset in front of friends, saying how hard it was to see Chris with someone else.'

It seemed Chris and Jennifer were openly flirtatious with each other at the party, and despite her best efforts at putting a brave face on the situation, Alexa was thought to be upset by the vibe at the event: 'Chris and Jennifer were really tactile with each other, which left Alexa feeling even more hurt,' an insider added. 'She tried to say hello to him while Jennifer was talking to other friends but told her pals it was really awkward.'

Days later Chris and Jennifer were out again, this time

sharing an intimate dinner at trendy Hollywood hotspot Chateau Marmont.

'The better she gets to know him, the more she likes him, she says he's super funny and sweet.'

Despite spending as much time as she possibly could with the Coldplay lead singer, Jennifer refused to ditch her female friends and did her best to carry on with her normal life. Just days before their date at Chateau Marmont, she came under fire for making an obscene hand gesture while out celebrating a friend's birthday. At a party for Lauren Ash, she was snapped by actress Rebel Wilson, who posted the photo on her Instagram account, leading to widespread comments about how different party-loving Jen is to Chris's clean-living ex-wife Gwyneth.

Jennifer also enjoyed nights out with award-winning singer Adele – the two were spotted out together, grabbing a bite to eat at exclusive Craig's restaurant in West Hollywood. According to *Just Jared*, they looked like they were having a great time as they caught up over dinner while sitting in a corner booth: 'Adele and Jen were both in very good spirits the whole night,' a source told the website. 'They were both wearing heels and dressed in head-to-toe black. Jen wore her hair down in a straight bob and looked super cute!'

Stacey Kubasak, Dior's director of Entertainment Relations, and a male companion, joined the high-profile pair.

Days later Jennifer and Chris were spotted enjoying a candlelit dinner date at Madeo, a swanky restaurant in Los Angeles. They arrived through the back door but dined in the main restaurant for two hours and ordered several items from the menu. The pair shared a mille-feuille dessert, and an onlooker said that the two were seen 'giggling' and 'laughing' during their date and seemed delighted with each other.

A source told the *New York Post*'s *Page Six* column: 'They were totally into each other. The romance is on, for sure.'

Another onlooker told *People*: 'They looked happy and just focused on each other. They were smiling, talking and very friendly.

'Even though they are both busy, the relationship is solid. They see each other when they can. Jennifer understands that the children come first with Chris and his relationship with Gwyneth is based around the family and it will always be a part of his life,' the insider continued. 'Things are good between them.'

Their unexpected decision to step out into the spotlight followed Gwyneth seemingly giving their relationship her stamp of approval during a series of revealing interviews, which led to Jennifer feeling more comfortable about taking things to the next level: 'Jen took Gwyneth's comments as the green light to go public with their relationship. She's persuading Chris to make things official,' a source told *Closer*. 'She's tired of sneaking around trying to keep it a secret – it's making her feel as if their relationship is controversial or she's doing something wrong. She's now keen to show the world she and Chris are an item.'

When asked about their relationship Gwyneth told Howard

Stern's *SiriusXM* radio show: 'Who says I don't approve [of Jennifer]? Why not? Why is it going to be an issue?

'I respect him as the father of my children. It's his life and it's his decision and I do think that he loves the kids so much and I don't think that he wouldn't be with someone who isn't great. And if I'm wrong, I'll come back here and tell you.'

Explaining her friendship with Chris, she went on: 'The idea is you try to do it with minimal acrimony and you say, "Look, we have kids, we're always going to be a family and let's try to find all the positives in our relationship, all the things that brought us together, the friendship."

'He's lovely,' she added. 'He's such a sweetheart. We actually have a really strong friendship and we laugh and we have fun.

'But there are times when it's really difficult and things happen and you're like, "I'm sure he doesn't want to hang out with me and I don't want to hang out with him". But for the sake of the kids you do it. But you also don't do it all tense.'

When asked how 'consciously uncoupling' works, Gwyneth explained: 'It's a very noble idea, it is kind of a goofy term. You say, "I really want to find my love for you, and I want to forgive you and I want you to forgive me, and let's have some fun as a family." Because, you know, he's going to be in my life for the rest of my life.

'When I was talking to friends of mine who had grown up and their parents were divorced, there was a common thread which was, "Oh yeah, now my parents are great and they were both at my wedding, but there was five years where they didn't talk", or "There were seven years where they wouldn't be in the same room." And I was like, "Can we just skip that?" Because I don't want to do that to my kids.'

She added: 'We're lucky in that our parenting styles and philosophies overlap a lot. We see eye to eye on how to do it.'

Stern then asked Gwyneth how she would she feel if he dated Rihanna. 'She's cool,' she responded.

When asked about actress Lindsay Lohan, Gwyneth replied: 'There's redemption, people get their acts together.'

She also talked about her famous relationship with Brad Pitt, saying: 'I definitely fell in love with him. He was so gorgeous and sweet. I mean, he was Brad Pitt! I was such a kid, I was twenty-two when we met. It's taken me until forty to get my head out of my ass.

'You can't make that decision when you're twenty-two years old. I wasn't ready, and he was too good for me. I didn't know what I was doing.'

Within days of Gwyneth appearing to give their relationship the thumbs up, Chris and Jennifer seemed more relaxed about appearing in public. And there were even suggestions that they had never actually split up at all, but had somehow managed to keep their meetings very private in the hope that people would lose interest.

Celeb Buzz reported: 'Sources close to [Jen and Chris] are revealing they never actually broke up in the first place. They just wanted the public to *think* they did.'

Despite Gwyneth appearing to be relaxed about it, there were also contradicting reports that privately she was not happy about Chris moving on, so he was perhaps being cautious and respectful towards his ex-wife. 'Chris feels torn – he knows he could risk losing Jen if he doesn't make it official soon, but he's told her he is trying to tread carefully for Gwyneth's sake,' an insider explained. 'It seems he isn't sure if she's ready to watch him and Jen become Hollywood's newest couple.'

As *The Stir* reported: 'Apparently, Chris and Jen have even found a way for him to visit her Los Angeles home when he's in town without anyone finding out. Considering how swift the paparazzi are – they're basically ninjas with cameras – this is quite a feat on their part. I imagine both have a pretty solid support system built around them and that their people are damn good at keeping secrets.'

Meanwhile *Radar Online* claimed that Chris was so smitten that he wanted Jennifer to meet Apple and Moses. 'Chris has fallen hard for Jen, and they are having a lot of fun together,' a source told the website. 'It's happened very fast, and it's extremely intense. Apple and Moses haven't met their dad's girlfriend, yet. Chris hasn't been discussing the relationship with Gwyneth, out of respect.

'It won't be happening right away, Chris wants to make sure this relationship is not going to just fizzle out before taking such a big step.

'He sees this relationship going the distance,' the source added. 'But it seems he isn't sure if Gwyneth was ready to watch him and Jen become Hollywood's newest couple.'

By that stage, Jennifer had not even met Gwyneth, and she deliberately stayed away from the 2015 Oscars because

Gwyneth wanted to go, and they wanted to avoid an awkward encounter on the red carpet.

'Chris hasn't wanted them to meet just yet,' a friend of Jennifer's told *Us Weekly*. 'Gwyneth and Chris are co-parenting without Jen involved for now.'

Meanwhile *Gossip Cop* suggested that Gwyneth did not want Jennifer around her children, but Chris was waiting for the right time to introduce them, adding that he was the one putting the brakes on a potential meeting date. But *Celebrity Dish* fuelled the rumours that all was not as harmonious as it appeared, by reporting: 'According to the latest report from *Naughty Gossip*, Jennifer Lawrence has "demands" for Chris Martin.

'More specifically, Jennifer has ordered Chris to stay away from his ex-wife, Gwyneth Paltrow, not see her, not talk to her, and basically have the most limited interaction with her as possible. Obviously, they are raising two children together, so a complete cut-off isn't possible.

'*Naughty Gossip*'s sources add that Chris apparently isn't taking Jennifer's demands seriously, and he thinks they're all rooted in jealousy and insecurity.'

If the situation already seemed confusing to outsiders, the rumour mill went into overdrive on Valentine's weekend in February 2015, when Chris decided to spend the romantic holiday with his ex-wife instead of Jennifer, prompting yet more speculation that a reconciliation might be on the cards. The estranged couple spent the day on the beach with Moses and Apple. They even walked arm in arm along the sands, as their Maltese dog, Daffodil, lingered behind, in what appeared to be the epitome of a happy family scene.

The famous couple also brought along actress Kate Hudson's young son Ryder, who is friends with Moses. Jennifer, meanwhile, was thousands of miles away in Boston, where she was seen having dinner with friends, including producer John Davis at Scampo, a restaurant in the Liberty Hotel.

It was suggested at this point that Chris was hopeful of a reunion. According to *Grazia*: 'He has been jumping through hoops to make it happen in the last year, including doing "homework" by reading stacks of self-help books suggested by Gwyneth to help him "actualise" himself. He's written her love songs, and has put his relationship with Jen on hold more than once.'

According to the magazine, the singer's efforts were paying off. 'Gwyneth has always made it clear there's a hope that they could get back together. They even decided to postpone the official divorce indefinitely, but it's only in the last few weeks that she's seemed keen to become a couple again.

'It was at her suggestion that they spend Valentine's Day together.

'Neither of them gave much weight to the occasion itself, but obviously she felt it would be a nice gesture for the kids, and it looks like she's testing the waters for a full-blown reunion. They seem closer than ever right now.

'Chris has made it clear to Jen that Gwyneth and his family are his priority, and they're keeping things casual while it works itself out.'

But then, just a couple of weeks later, Chris was back on the beach with Kate Hudson, who was laughing at his jokes and wearing a very skimpy Mara Hoffman bikini. She had been single since breaking off her engagement with Muse frontman Matt Bellamy and briefly dating *Dancing With The Stars* pro Derek Hough. Later that evening the pair were seen at a restaurant, with Kate's son Bingham: 'The children are already mates. Kate has a lot of the qualities Chris liked about Gwyneth – she's a great cook and family is very important to her – but she is very different in a way he likes, too.

'She's very laid-back and funny, basically a combination of Jen and Gwyn,' an insider told British magazine *Heat*. 'Kate's fancied Chris for ages. They've been friends for years, but she was with Matt Bellamy.

'In October, Chris went to Kate's Hallowe'en party and everyone was talking about their chemistry. Then, she broke up with Matt just before Christmas, but Chris was with Jennifer. Now, the timing is finally perfect.

'It's not like Gwyn wants him back, but she doesn't want him dating one of their good friends.'

In Touch also reported Chris's shock move in their April edition: 'Since Kate and Matt split last fall, she's been clingy with Chris, calling him all the time to suggest get-togethers under the guise of setting up play dates for the kids – which is exactly how the beach day and dinner date came to be,' a source told the magazine. 'Kate knew Gwyneth and Jennifer were out of town, so she took the opportunity to make a major play for Chris.'

Meanwhile *Star* magazine reported that Chris had turned to Kate after Jennifer gave him an ultimatum – divorce his wife or end their relationship. Apparently he chose his marriage over Jennifer, and then found himself another woman who appeared not to mind that he and Gwyneth were not yet divorced.

According to the 30 March 2015 edition of *Star*, Chris and Kate had been dating in secret for weeks: 'The couple, who weren't shy about shamelessly flirting in front of the paparazzi, turned their day date into a family affair. Kate brought along sons Ryder and Bingham, while Chris brought his kids Apple and Moses. Showing up together on the beach was their way of going public with their relationship, they knew they would attract attention.'

The suggestion of a blossoming romance between Chris and Kate apparently came as another major blow to Gwyneth, who was reportedly so devastated that she embarked on an extreme diet and exercise regime.

'Gwyneth prides herself on having a better body now than when she was twenty-two, but seeing that Chris is dating someone so young has made her really want to make sure she's in top shape,' a source told *Radar*. 'It's not even for him. It's for her, but she needs to feel like she is better looking than anyone else he could ever date. She's relentless about her figure.'

Friends feared the actress was losing touch with reality: 'Her friends are on midlife crisis alert,' an insider told *Heat* magazine. 'No one in Hollywood is more competitive than her. She's also taking more risks with her fashion to try and look younger,' said the source.

And *Grazia* magazine reported that it had ruined Kate and Gwyneth's friendship – they had grown close when they both lived in London with their British rocker husbands. 'Gwyneth feels like this is a betrayal. She and Kate used to be very close but their friendship has cooled in recent years. To see Kate and Chris getting on so well is hard for her,' a source told the magazine. 'Kate and Chris have always had a great relationship but there's definitely chemistry between them now. Kate is relaxed and easy going, which Chris loves, while Kate's really into her music – she's a sucker for a musician. They enjoy spending time together.'

But Chris and Kate's public outings left things rather awkward for their mutual friendship group: 'Gwyneth is devastated that Chris is spending so much time with someone she once considered a good friend,' reported *Grazia*. 'It's not lost on her that they all used to hang out together, and Kate and Gwyneth have mutual friends like Stella McCartney and Liv Tyler, so there's a lot of tension in the circle right now.

'Kate and Chris wouldn't have gone public with the children if they weren't confident about their friendship – they've both been very good at keeping their families out of the spotlight in the past.'

According to the website *Design&Trend*, Jennifer was determined to win Chris back, though, with an insider adding that she 'won't go down without a fight'.

'Jen's just not going to let this happen,' said a source. 'She's invested a lot of time into making this relationship work.'

Of course Jennifer was free to date other people as well,

and around the same time it emerged that she was still in contact with her old boyfriend, Nicholas Hoult. According to a February 2015 edition of OK! magazine: 'Jen reaches out to Nicholas Hoult all of the time for advice and emotional support.'

A friend of Jennifer's explained: 'If Chris can keep in touch with Gwyneth Paltrow then why can't she lean on Nick? She's hedging her bets and playing a bit of a game. She realises there are no guarantees and wants to keep Nick in the picture.'

Various sources claimed she had been growing close to her ex-boyfriend again, with another revealing: 'Their relationship is getting closer and his family would love for them to get back together. He still adores Jennifer and so do his family.

'He's been calling her and they've been speaking regularly on Skype.'

Jennifer was also being romantically linked to her co-star Josh Hutcherson. Within days of the speculation, he appeared to be dating Glee actress Dianna Agron, though. They were seen dancing together at a party held at Los Angeles pop-up club Bungalow 8, while rapper Diplo performed. 'Diplo came out unplanned and Josh hit the dance floor with Dianna,' reported Page Six. 'They both love to dance and have a good time. They looked like a new couple, still flirting.'

However, E! News reported that nothing romantic happened between them. 'There was no PDA, flirting or kissing,' an insider told E! And according to J-14, Josh was actually dating his co-star from Escobar: Paradise Lost (2014), Claudia Traisac.

By a bizarre coincidence Dianna was later linked to

Nicholas Hoult, after they were spotted together in a string of low-key London pubs in April 2015. Apparently Nicholas was showing her his favourite places, and they were even seen kissing in a pub in West Hampstead over Easter. A source told *The Sun*: 'No one thought much about it but recently they've become very close and are behaving quite couply. They've been friends for a long time. It's early days but things between them are ticking along nicely.'

And a source told *People* magazine: 'They came in with each other and ordered some drinks. They sat down and had a conversation just like everyone else.

'They seemed like they had a nice time, but we didn't see them kissing. But then, we were working, so we weren't really looking.

'It was definitely them. Both of them are very beautiful, so it's difficult to miss them,' the source added. 'They weren't flirting or kissing or anything. It wasn't like they were a couple. Maybe they were just getting to know each other.'

To add to the web of confusion, Jennifer, Josh and Liam were spotted out for dinner together in early March. The three *Hunger Games* co-stars met up at Italian restaurant Locanda Verde in New York.

Jennifer was also linked to Luke Hemmings, of the band 5 Seconds of Summer, after he admitted that he admired her. He told *Top of the Pops* magazine: 'If I could spread a rumour about myself, it would be that Jennifer Lawrence and I are dating. Even though that's never going to happen.'

At this stage, despite all the confusion and conflicting

rumours, slowly the gossip began to die down and it gradually became clear that Chris and Kate Hudson were just friends; he was in fact still dating Jennifer, and would soon be divorcing Gwyneth.

In an interview with *Marie Claire Australia* in February 2015, Gwyneth had shed more light on her split from Chris, confirming that the marriage was very much over: 'There was nothing dramatic or anything,' she said. 'I had built my life on trying to be all things to all people, and I just couldn't do it anymore, and I really had the sense that I wasn't allowed to have needs, and I had to prove my specialness or self-worth by doing all this stuff and taking care of everybody else, and I just sort of hit a wall.

'We've worked really fucking hard to get to [this] point. But we're very, very close, and it's so nice.

'I feel like it's, in a way, the relationship we were meant to have.'

Meanwhile Chris and Jennifer still managed to snatch occasional dates together, which was easier said than done, given that their work commitments often kept them on opposite sides of the country.

While Jennifer was filming in Boston in the spring of 2015 they had just enough time to squeeze in a romantic weekend in New York, where they shared brunch at the exclusive Tavern on The Green restaurant. While bodyguards kept over-zealous photographers at bay, Jennifer tucked into a roast beef sandwich and Chris enjoyed eggs Benedict, before they strolled together through Central Park: 'It was an affectionate and romantic date for Chris and Jen,' reported *OK!* magazine. 'They were whispering to each other and giggling.

'They see each other when they can, yet each continues to do their own thing. Both have full plates, and they like it that way.'

And it seemed Jennifer was so determined to impress Chris that she even began to tone down her goofy persona. A source told *Celeb Dirty Laundry*: 'Chris is conservative, especially in social settings and it has rubbed off on Jen, who is learning to keep some things private.'

But they only had a day together in New York before he flew off to Puerto Vallarta in Mexico with Gwyneth and their children to celebrate their son Moses' ninth birthday. They were seen on the beach, looking like any normal happy family, although Gwyneth had been pictured days earlier attending Robert Downey Junior's 50th birthday party with her boyfriend, Brad Falchuk.

However, it appeared Chris and Gwyneth were at last heading towards finalising their divorce, a year after announcing their split. *TMZ* reported their 'divorce mediator is working towards a property and custody settlement, and once it's a done deal, the petition for divorce will be filed.'

And an insider confirmed to the *Daily Mail*: 'A divorce is definitely 100 per cent on. They are working out a deal privately and there will be no leaks. This is a very amicable break-up and the resolution is near.

'Papers will be filed soon and the divorce will be dealt with quickly. They both love their children and they still have the utmost respect for each other. But they are not getting back together.'

Insiders suggested that Jennifer had been putting pressure on Chris to push ahead with his divorce, and that had been discussed at their surprisingly public brunch date in New York: 'Chris and Jennifer had been struggling to move forward with their relationship because she couldn't handle always coming second to Gwyneth,' reported *Grazia* magazine in April. 'She put a huge amount of pressure on Chris to make a statement to show his commitment to her, which he wasn't prepared to do until now.

'They [Chris and Gwyneth] decided to finally bite the bullet, with the support of their conscious uncoupling guru. They both felt the time had come to move forward with their new relationships.'

However, although the papers were ready to be signed, divorce would not signal the end of their close relationship, as the pair were determined to continue to spend time together with their children. 'They have been using their business managers to work out a settlement agreement involving both property and custody,' reported the *Daily Mail*. 'The settlement is confidential but insiders claim there were no big problems with money or custody of their two children.'

The official documents were expected to cite irreconcilable differences between the pair, who married on 5 December 2003. 'They've decided to draw up a "family schedule", which they will both have to adhere to once the divorce is finalised,' added the *Daily Mail*'s insider. 'It will include at least three family holidays a year, designated joint days out with the kids and even "date nights" to discuss the children and remain on good terms.'

And *People* magazine reported that the couple would continue to focus on ensuring their children were as happy as possible: 'This is a natural evolution for Gwyneth and Chris as friends and as a couple,' a source told the magazine. 'They remain close, and they remain totally committed to Apple and Moses – as they find their way forward as individuals, they will naturally be more public about seeing other people, if not showy about it.'

Whoever Jennifer eventually ends up with, it seems likely that having children will be high on her list of priorities. She remains as close as ever to her tight-knit family and, after playing bridesmaid when her brother Blaine married his girlfriend Carson Massier in October 2013, she went on to be a very doting aunt when their son Theodore was born in September 2014. Perhaps playing 'mother' might prove to be her most challenging role to date?

CHAPTER TWELVE

THE FUTURE'S BRIGHT

As one of the most popular, not to mention bankable, stars in Hollywood, Jennifer now finds herself in the luxurious position of being able to cherry-pick from the finest roles that come her way. While other actresses her age fight to get themselves noticed by casting directors, she is inundated with acting offers and product endorsement contracts on a daily basis, but she is just as happy to turn many of them down. Unconcerned by money, she takes great care to make considered choices that are good for her long-term career.

Deep down, she is not truly interested in raising her profile by attending parties, or even key industry events, preferring to focus on her work. At the start of 2015 Jennifer even ducked out of the high-profile Golden Globes and Academy Awards, instead choosing to spend the awards season filming on the East Coast.

Some commentators suggested at the time that she was avoiding Gwyneth Paltrow, who made a glamorous appearance at the Golden Globes, presenting the Best Actor Award to Eddie Redmayne for his role as Professor Stephen Hawking in *The Theory of Everything*.

The same night as the Golden Globes took place, Jennifer was focusing very much on her career – she was spotted dining with crew from her film *Joy*, released December 2015, at the popular Bricco North End restaurant in Boston. According to Bricco's PR rep, Nicole Russo, the star ordered the branzino fish and was 'down to earth and nice to the staff'.

She was in the city for much of the spring of 2015, working on her third project led by *Silver Linings Playbook* and *American Hustle* director David O. Russell. It seems hard to imagine now that have such a successful working partnership that the director has since confessed he was not at all impressed by Jennifer on first meeting her at an American Film Institute lunch several years earlier.

'She looked kind of like an Orange County girl,' he told *The Hollywood Reporter* in 2014. 'All dressed up in a white dress with big hair, with high heels. And I was like, "Who is that? That's the girl from *Winter's Bone*?" I said, "Wow, she doesn't look anything like that." Then [later in 2011], she did a Skype audition that blew me away.'

That audition would win the actress the role of Tiffany in *Silver Linings Playbook* – and ultimately an Oscar. Reunited once again in 2015, Jennifer and Russell were working together on *Joy*, a film which tells the true story of Joy

Mangano, a struggling single mother living on Long Island, who found great success as an unlikely businesswoman when she created the Miracle Mop.

A statement released by 20th Century Fox regarding the upcoming film, read: 'Written and directed by acclaimed filmmaker, David O. Russell, *Joy* is the emotionally compelling and often comedic journey of a woman who triumphed over personal and financial challenges by inventing the Miracle Mop, which she sold on QVC and went on to become a hugely successful entrepreneur.'

The movie also saw Jennifer reunited with her former co-stars Bradley Cooper and Robert De Niro. But she was forced to publicly deny allegations that she and her director got embroiled in a huge argument on set. She took the highly unusual step of using her official Facebook page – which she hardly ever updates personally – to address reports that they had been heard shouting at each other, writing: 'Hey guys! It's Jen! I know I don't go on here a lot because I can barely work email but there's been a terrible rumour going around the last twenty-four hours so I wanted to clear it up.

'David O. Russell is one of my closest friends and we have an amazing collaborative working relationship. I adore this man and he does not deserve this tabloid malarkey. This movie is going great and I'm having a blast making it!' she declared.

The actress's announcement came after a source told *TMZ* that she and Russell were loudly screaming and swearing at each other on set. The website alleged that the argument began because Jennifer was unhappy with how he was directing a scene. But producers told *TMZ* that the screaming – which apparently scared onlookers – was simply method acting as he was helping Jennifer to get riled up before they shot a scene in which she had to lose her temper at another actor.

TMZ also alleged that Jennifer had invited studio boss Harvey Weinstein on to the set to discuss the problem, but that Russell had ordered him to leave as soon as he reached her make-up trailer. Later it emerged that the meeting had been pre-arranged, and was nothing to do with the supposed argument. It was also confirmed that both actress and director were aware that Weinstein was due to visit, and that he went to see Jennifer to discuss a project with her for an hour, also presenting her with a handbag from his girlfriend's fashion label, Marchesa.

Meanwhile, Fox 2000's representative confirmed that Russell had an argument with a different Fox executive, but denied reports that he made the woman cry. And the head of the production company Annapurna Pictures also weighed in on the feud: 'The only thing happening on set between David Russell and Jennifer Lawrence is an extraordinary collaboration,' explained Megan Ellison. 'One I'm proud to be a part of.'

Either way, the long-running and fruitful artistic relationship between Jennifer and Russell looked set to continue, although it was not the first time he had allegedly argued with an actor in one of his movies. He famously fell out with George Clooney on the set of 1999's *Three Kings* – they criticised each other's work openly, and even got into a physical fight.

Footage also surfaced in 2004 of the director and Lily Tomlin screaming at each other while working on *I Heart Huckabees* – with Russell knocking over props and Tomlin swearing at him. The actress told the *Miami New Times* three years later: 'I love David. There was a lot of pressure in making the movie – even the way it came out, you could see it was a very free-associative, crazy movie, and David was under a tremendous amount of pressure. And he's a very free-form kind of guy anyway.'

A couple of months later, however, Russell's reputation was further damaged in a spate of leaked emails sent between journalist Jonathan Alter and the director's brother-in-law, Sony CEO Michael Lynton. In the emails, Alter enquires as to the company's future plans with the director: 'Are you guys doing anything else with him?' Alter asks. 'I know he's brilliant but we have someone on our show who worked closely with him on *American Hustle* and not only are the stories about him reforming himself total bullshit but the new stories of his abuse and lunatic behavior are extreme even by Hollywood standards.'

Alter brought up the feud with George Clooney, adding: 'Apparently he behaved on *The Fighter* but acted so crazy on *Hustle* that it's another Clooney situation where a lot of people won't work with him again.

'He grabbed one guy by the collar, cursed out people repeatedly in front of others and so abused Amy Adams that Christian Bale got in his face and told him to stop acting like an asshole.

'He treated the crew like shit, demanded his own bathroom at all times and frightened people, as he famously had on *Three Kings*.'

Whatever the rumours regarding the talented director, he and Jennifer have clearly struck up a prolific and fruitful professional relationship which has already spawned two fantastic films in *Silver Linings Playbook* and *American Hustle* – and more is on the horizon.

Joy was expected to go head to head with Sandra Bullock's rival biopic of another groundbreaking woman, Tupperware promoter Brownie Wise, who famously inspired housewives to earn their own money through Tupperware parties. Both she and Joy Mangano were trailblazing businesswomen who reached the top of their professions through hard work, talent and charisma. By coincidence, their unusual life stories were being brought to the big screen in separate films, which earlier in 2015 was being billed as the Battle of the Domestic Goddesses.

Bullock's film is based on the book *Tupperware Unsealed*, written by Bob Kealing, in which he explained how Earl Tupper developed the food storage containers, applying for a patent in 1947. Tupper was at a loss as to how to market the products and discovered Wise, a divorcée and mother, who had a prodigious talent for selling and was a 'dazzling, intelligent and outgoing woman'. In the postwar baby boom she set up parties for stay-at-home mothers, showing them how to 'burp' the lid to force air out of the colourful bowls and create a vacuum. Sales took off, as previously women had had to resort to putting shower caps over dishes to prevent food from spoiling. Throughout the 1950s, thousands of women became Tupperware hostesses, rewarded with incentives that ranged from sets of steak knives to Cadillacs and mink coats. In 1954, Wise was the first woman to appear on the cover of *Business Week* magazine, when the company's estimated sales had reached $100 million.

But Tupper came to resent his employee's success; in 1957 Wise was fired from the multimillion-dollar company she had helped build. She held no company stock and was given a pay-off of a year's salary of $30,000. Afterwards she tried – and failed – to start a cosmetics company, dabbled in property and had a pottery studio. In 1992 she died at the age of seventy-nine.

'She was one of the most important businesswomen of the twentieth century, the prototype for all these Facebook and Google women who are leaning in,' wrote Kealing. 'I'm glad she will finally get the recognition she deserves.'

Joy Mangano's rags-to-riches story is equally uplifting. The former waitress used her own savings to develop a mop that could be wrung out without the user getting their hands wet. In 1990 she made 100 mops and sold them to shops in Long Island. She sold a further 1,000 mops to the *QVC* shopping channel, on condition that she would take them back if they did not sell. The mops moved slowly but when Mangano went on air to sell the product herself, she sold 18,000 mops in twenty minutes. Today, they still sell by the million.

The blonde and bubbly Mangano also invented Huggable

Hangers, which save space in wardrobes, and she broke a selling record on the *Home Shopping Network* in 2010 by selling 180,000 of her Forever Fragrant air fresheners in a single day.

She sold her company, Ingenious Designs, to HSN and now works there as an executive. Her daughter, Christie Miranne, told the *Observer* that her mother was 'excited and honoured' to be portrayed by Jennifer Lawrence. 'She's worked really hard all her life. We're all looking forward to seeing the film. It's going to be quite an experience,' she said.

Some critics are sceptical that the two women's life stories, which include their complicated love lives, will be strong enough to draw audiences but others believe they will be hits, with cinemagoers weary of non-stop action and fantasy films.

Jennifer, meanwhile, seemed to settle into life in Boston, and was spotted trying to live life as normally as any Hollywood actress could. She went shopping at Saks Fifth Avenue, and somehow managed to slip unnoticed into a Flywheel exercise class: 'She normally sneaks in the back door, walks into class late after the lights go down, and sneaks out early before they go on,' a source told *People* magazine. She attended the class with her assistant, and even brought her dog Pippi, who waited patiently outside the class. 'When she brings her dog, which she has done a few times, her bodyguard watches him,' added the source.

From Boston the production moved on to Wilmington, Massachusetts, where Jennifer was spotted filming alongside her co-star Édgar Ramírez. And she told friends she was delighted to be teaming up with Bradley Cooper once again, as the smouldering chemistry between the pair was undeniable and had delighted critics in their previous movies.

Jennifer had also formed a close friendship with Bradley's then girlfriend, British model Suki Waterhouse. Bradley and Suki first met at the 2013 Elle Style Awards in London: 'We were introduced and hit it off almost immediately,' the model told *Rollercoaster* magazine. 'We were dancing at the after-party, and he asked me if I fancied going to a club. We went to Cirque le Soir in London – and he's a ridiculously good dancer.'

Suki struck up a friendship with Jennifer, and together the two women went to watch Cooper's Broadway debut in *The Elephant Man* in December 2014.

In the revival of Bernard Pomerance's drama at the Booth Theatre, Cooper played Joseph Merrick, a nineteenth-century British man who becomes the star of the travelling freak show circuit. A fellow theatre-goer excitedly tweeted during the performance: 'Jennifer Lawrence is sitting across the row from us at *The Elephant Man*', with several shocked face emojis following it. And Jennifer's appearance at the theatre sparked speculation that she might have plans to take to the stage herself, if her filming commitments would allow it.

Although the two women appeared quite friendly that night, it has also been reported that Jennifer was a 'little jealous' of Suki. A source told gossip website *Radar Online*: 'When Bradley and Jennifer made *Silver Linings Playbook* and *Serena* together they were inseparable. But now Bradley has been spending his free time with Suki, and she feels like she's lost her partner in crime.

'They haven't been hanging around each other as often as they used to.

'Bradley flew Suki over from London to Boston and he took her on a tour of the city. Then, he flew to Paris to see her the moment he had a break in filming.

'Because he's spending all his free time with Suki, Jennifer's only really seen Bradley on set and she's grown a little jealous about it.'

Bradley and Jennifer had been forced to deny rumours they were dating, but it was not the most convincing denial as he claimed Jennifer was too young for him – before going on to date Suki, who was even younger!

Jennifer had previously claimed she was tired of trying to arrange dates for Bradley. 'I feel like all I've been doing lately is setting him up,' she said. 'I was like, "You know what? I'm gonna save time and just get you a booklet with pictures of my friends. You just go through and pick them out, because this is getting exhausting."'

And while she kept away from the Oscars in 2015, Bradley took Suki as his date, following his nomination for Best Actor in *American Sniper*. As well as losing out on the night to Eddie Redmayne, he also had to put up with Suki feeling jealous about another of his gorgeous female friends. According to *OK!* magazine, Bradley's girlfriend had some negative feelings towards actress Sienna Miller, who made a glamorous appearance at the Academy Awards, looking stunning in a black Oscar de la Renta dress.

A source told the magazine: 'Suki is so fed up with Bradley's relentless gushing about Sienna's talent, it has caused some huge fights. Suki told him that if she walks by Sienna at the Oscars, she is going to tell her to stay away from her man.'

Since Bradley had been romantically linked to Sienna in the past, it was perhaps understandable that Suki should be annoyed, especially as the couple hardly spent any time together in the run-up to the high-profile awards ceremony. However, the model refused to discuss their relationship. During an interview with *Elle* magazine she said: 'I don't talk about my boyfriend because it's boring. At least, that's what I decided to tell you when you asked. I'm not one of those girls who goes on about their boyfriends. I do think whatever I say will sound weird. But the truth is, if I start talking about him, I probably won't be able to stop. And I don't really want to talk about him, you know?'

But in April 2015 it emerged that Bradley had cooled his two-year relationship with Suki because she was not supportive of his career. *Page Six* claimed that he felt neglected during his Broadway stint in *The Elephant Man* between November 2014 and February 2015. The column also reported that a source close to the actor said that Bradley was upset that Suki chose not to spend Valentine's Day with him in New York, preferring instead to enjoy a girls' weekend away in Texas – sharing on Instagram a series of photos of herself in bikinis.

Bradley also had professional problems. In the spring of 2015 fans were eagerly anticipating the delayed release of *Serena*, based on the 2008 novel of the same name by Ron Rash and directed by Oscar-winner Susanne Bier. Jennifer and Bradley play a couple whose happiness is almost ruined when Lawrence's character finds out that her husband already has a child. The film's release was delayed for almost two years while it languished in the editing suite and when it finally came out in March 2015, it was to terrible reviews.

The movie, set in the early 1920s, follows two newlyweds, George and Serena Pemberton (Bradley Cooper and Jennifer Lawrence), who found a timber business in the North Carolina mountains. Serena proves herself a formidable outdoors-woman, hunting rattlesnakes and even saving a man's life in the wilderness (a rough-and-tumble role harking back to Jennifer's breakout role in *Winter's Bone*). Yet their marriage begins to unravel as Serena discovers George's hidden past and is forced to face up to an unchangeable fate of her own.

Although the film itself was slated, some critics praised Jennifer's performance, and credited Susanne Bier with bringing out the best in her. 'Lawrence constructs a well considered and thought out performance that makes sense of the character's extremes,' wrote the *Houston Chronicle*. 'At times, you can feel Bier relishing what this actress is capable of, as when she films Lawrence in close-up, reacting to bad news in one unbroken take. Her face is still, then she starts to cry, and then her face gives way to sobbing. Very few people are capable of doing this with a camera two feet from their face. Even fewer could make you want to watch.'

According to Sony's head of acquisitions Joe Matukewicz the film was 'very disappointing'. He wrote in a leaked email to his boss: 'It's set in a logging town in the Smoky Mountains of the 1920s. Cooper runs a timber company, marries Lawrence, but after she loses their unborn baby she mentally unravels, having three locals killed who she perceives as threats. Even with this star power, the bleak story, setting, tedious pacing and tonally challenged film make it one we should steer clear of. Not only because the reviews will be rough, but also for the talent relationships.

'It's probably best to let it go.'

The website *Zimbio* also slammed the film as 'a yawn', saying: 'The movie's best moments feature Lawrence in emotional overload. One, where she slowly breaks down after the miscarriage, is filmed in tight close-up and will send chills down your spine. This is what's so frustrating. *Serena* should be full of moments like this, but Lawrence is only given half a character.

'Meanwhile, Bier lays it on with heavy strings and slow motion. This passes for character development. The long, soulful looks between Lawrence and Cooper add little and the film's PG-rated sex scenes are a yawn.

'Filmed mainly in Prague, the production design is stellar and vivid, a hard vision of a worker's life. And it seems like the environment affected the film.

'Apart from Lawrence, the actors all look like they'd rather be home in bed, like they knew they were working on something that wasn't working.'

Despite the mixed reviews that plagued *Serena*, Jennifer and Bradley were still widely considered to be box-office gold and even though this particular film proved a rare flop, it is safe to say that Jennifer's future in the movie business is guaranteed, since she is already set to be busy for years to come.

She forged a strong bond with the director and agreed to reunite with Susanne Bier again in the movie adaptation of Claire Bidwell Smith's memoir entitled *The Rules of Inheritance*. As well as starring, Jennifer also intended to tackle producing for the first time in the film about coping with grief and the challenges that come with losing a loved one.

At the time of writing she was also set to take lead roles in the movies *Burial Rites*, *East of Eden*, *The Hunger Games: Mockingjay – Part 2* and *The Ends of the Earth*. For both *Burial Rites* and *East of Eden* – a remake of the 1955 film starring James Dean – she was teaming up again with *Hunger Games* director Gary Ross. In the second adaptation of a John Steinbeck's seminal novel *East of Eden* she was set to star as Cathy Ames, who murdered her parents by setting fire to their house while they slept.

In *Burial Rites* Jennifer was to play a woman charged with murder who is sent to a remote farm while she awaits execution.

For *The Ends of the Earth*, she was to be reunited with the director of the third and fourth instalments of the *Hunger Games* franchise, Francis Lawrence, for a fact-based love story about a powerful oil tycoon who loses everything after being caught up in a torrid affair.

And she and Francis Lawrence had plans to team up again for a romantic drama called *The Dive*. According to *The Hollywood Reporter* the film, which *Avatar* and *Titanic* director

James Cameron has been developing since 2002, centres on the relationship between true-life figures Francisco 'Pipin' Ferreras and marine biologist Audrey Mestre.

Jennifer will play Audrey, a scuba diving enthusiast who became interested in the sport of free diving (which involves diving to the greatest depths on a single breath of air) in the mid-nineties. She trained under, and later married, the legendary free diver, Pipin. In November 2002, while attempting to break the world record dive of 531 feet set earlier by her husband – without breathing apparatus – Audrey encountered an issue with a lift balloon. Pulled from the water nine minutes later, efforts to resuscitate her were unsuccessful and she died at the age of twenty-eight.

Two very different accounts of the tragedy have since emerged. In 2006 Pipin was directly blamed for his wife's untimely death by dive co-organiser Carlos Serra in his book called *The Last Attempt*, amid allegations the record attempt failed to adhere to standard safety procedures. However, the film follows the title of Pipin's own 2004 book, *The Dive: A Story of Love and Obsession*, which takes a different view.

Jennifer also planned to take on more producing later in the year, and agreed to simultaneously produce and star in the film of *The Glass Castle*. In an interview with *The Associated Press* she said that her mother Karen had encouraged her to read the gripping life story of former gossip columnist Jeannette Walls.

Jennifer said: 'I've always wanted to produce, because I remember when I would read these incredible scripts that would never see the light of day and then I'd drive through Westwood and see some of the crap that was coming out. And I was like, "What is going on in the world?"

'So I've always wanted to produce. And *Glass Castle* being my first project is perfect because I was just so moved by that book. My mother is like the lucky charm with these kinds of things. She read *Winter's Bone* and *Hunger Games* and when I read *The Glass Castle* I thought it was amazing, so we found Gil Netter, the producer who had the rights to the book. He and I started talking and now we are developing. We have a director and a writer and it's getting going.'

And in 2016 Jennifer is scheduled to reprise her superhero role *in X-Men: Apocalypse*, playing the role of Raven/Mystique again. But she revealed that it would be her final appearance in the sci-fi series, having taken over the role from Rebecca Romijn. Speaking at a screening of *Serena* in March 2015, Jennifer confirmed: 'It is my last one, actually.' Nicholas Hoult had also indicated that the film would be his last outing as Beast, but he would continue if he had the choice.

Speaking to *E! Online*, Jennifer's former boyfriend revealed: 'This is the last one I'm signed up for. The first one did so well and *Days of Future Past* got received so brilliantly. It's like, "Wow, people really want to see the films", and the best thing is it's a great crew and cast to work with and he's a fun character. I have a good time playing him so I'd keep making them.'

After Jennifer announced she would be stepping down, and leaving the *X-Men* franchise for good, director Bryan Singer started the search for another main female lead. And in April 2015 he cast Olivia Munn to play the ninja telepath Psylocke in *X-Men: Apocalypse*. He made the announcement via Instagram, with Hollywood insiders immediately predicting Munn's career would rocket just as Jennifer's had done after appearing as Mystique in *X-Men: First Class*.

It was also reported that Jennifer and Chris Pratt – star of *Guardians of the Galaxy* and *The Lego Movie* – were in talks with Sony Pictures to board the upcoming sci-fi drama *Passengers*.

In fact *Passengers* has been in development for years and has yet to lock down its leads. Back in 2013, Rachel McAdams and Keanu Reeves were the rumoured stars, with *Game of Thrones* director Brian Kirk at the helm. Before that Reese Witherspoon was in talks with the studio. All three actors have since dropped out.

'*Passengers* is set on a spacecraft in the future, with thousands of passengers making an interstellar voyage to a distant new planet,' reported industry magazine *Variety* in early 2015. 'One passenger awakens from cryogenic sleep ninety years before anyone else and decides to wake up a female passenger, sparking the beginning of a love story.'

According to *Variety*, Morten Tyldum, who was behind Oscar-nominated drama *The Imitation Game* (2014), was hoping to land the directing job. Tyldum had been nominated for an Oscar and a Directors Guild award for his work on *The Imitation Game*, the Second World War period drama starring Benedict Cumberbatch as code-cracking hero Alan Turing.

Industry insiders hope that *Passengers* will echo the huge

box-office success of recent space dramas such as *Interstellar* (2014) and *Gravity* (2013) – the latter also being the recipient of seven Oscars.

Around this time Jennifer was being linked to so many films that there was widespread surprise that she was not considered for Paul Feig's upcoming remake of the *Ghostbusters'* movie, this time with an all-female cast.

True to form, Jennifer made a joke about the perceived snub: 'I didn't know there was a *Ghostbusters 2*. Who's in *2*? Are you serious? Oh, my God! Sequels are never as good,' she said, bursting into laughter when she realised that she was actually promoting a sequel at the time (the sequel being Mockingjay: Part 1).

But Jennifer was too busy to dwell on the one that got away; she was also due to team up with Hollywood legend Steven Spielberg for a biopic about a veteran war photographer. Warner Bros. Studio was hammering out a deal for her to star in the film version of the memoir *It's What I Do: A Photographer's Life of Love and War*.

Lynsey Addario penned the memoir about her assignments in conflict zones, including Afghanistan after the 9/11 terrorist attacks. According to *Deadline*, big-name producers were battling for the rights to the story after extracts were published in *The New York Times Magazine*. Bidders included Working Title Films, who had Reese Witherspoon attached to the lead role, and Darren Aronofsky (*Black Swan*), who wanted the movie for Natalie Portman. The Weinstein Company was also bidding, with George Clooney and Grant Heslov involved.

Margo Robbie, too, was reportedly hoping to buy the rights to the film.

The Pulitzer Prize-winning photojournalist had met with various hopeful bidders and impressed them all with details of her personal and professional life. Addario has covered conflicts in Afghanistan, Iraq, Darfur, the Congo and Haiti and her work has appeared in *The New York Times*, *The New York Times Magazine*, *Time*, *Newsweek* and *National Geographic*.

Warner Bros. eventually won the rights, casting Jennifer as Addario, who admitted she was concerned about Hollywood's tendency to sensationalise: 'That's why I went to great lengths to figure out who I would option the book with. I feel pretty confident about the team I've ended up going with. There's no guarantee it will be exactly the truth, but the goal for the movie is to tell people what it is that we do as journalists, what our lives are really like, and what the lives of the people we cover are really like.

'I think there's a great disparity between what people perceive and what the reality is, and if we can reach a much larger public with a Hollywood film, then let's try it.'

With an upcoming movie, Addario is now a wealthy woman, but Jennifer was impressed to learn that she has no plans to give up her dangerous job. Addario told the *British Journal of Photography*: 'It's hard for me when people ask "Why do you do this work, why would you risk your life?" I don't really have an intellectual answer, because anyone who does this work understands that it's beyond them, it's like a calling that overtakes you. The only thing I've come up with is, "It's what I do and it's who I am".'

There have been rumours linking Jennifer to a *Star Wars* spin-off project, as well as hints that she is set to play a video game heroine in *The Legend of Zelda*. And on the subject of princesses, another suggestion was that she would replace Kristen Bell in *Frozen 2*, following the success of her song, 'The Hanging Tree'.

And Jennifer is also being linked to future plans for a big-screen epic adaptation of *The Odyssey* being developed by Lionsgate films and possibly directed by Francis Lawrence.

She is even due to cash in on the opening of a *Hunger Games* theme park in Dubai. Lionsgate announced in April 2015 that it would be partnering Dubai Parks and Resorts to bring the film to life via a gigantic theme park scheduled to open in October 2016. Motiongate Dubai, a Hollywood-themed attraction, would feature *Hunger Games*-inspired attractions and retail facilities. The 4-million-square-foot facility is expected to attract more than 3 million visitors a year, and would include a live stage show and animation zone.

It was also reported that Jennifer would be playing Hearst publishing empire heiress-turned-activist Patty Hearst, who was kidnapped in 1974 by a student-led group called the Symbionese Liberation Army, who were campaigning for the release of black prisoners. In one of the most well-documented cases of Stockholm syndrome ever, Hearst was brainwashed into supporting her captors' cause, going on to appear in the group's propaganda videos and taking part in illegal activities.

She changed her name to Tania and fashioned herself as a machine-gun-toting guerilla warrior. But she was eventually arrested after staging an elaborate bank robbery to support her newfound cause. She was put on trial and later pardoned by President Jimmy Carter.

CNN senior legal analyst Jeffrey Toobin has written a so-far untitled book about Hearst's young life and 20th Century Fox is developing a screenplay with Jennifer in mind.

Critics suggested she would be perfect for the role since she had played a heroic warrior in *Hunger Games*, was emotionally vulnerable in *Silver Linings Playbook* and made a convincing sultry femme fatale in *American Hustle*.

If all this should come to pass, then it looks as though Jennifer will not be taking a break for a very long time to come.

Rolling Stone magazine declared Jennifer to be 'The most talented actress in America' and *Time* listed her as one of the 100 Most Influential People in the World.

Elle announced she was the Most Powerful Woman in the Entertainment Industry, and she found herself ranked Number 1 on *Ask Men*'s list of the Top 99 Most Desirable Women of the Year.

As well as all her other acting awards, gongs and trophies, Jennifer also found herself ranked by *Forbes* magazine as one of the World's Most Powerful Celebrities and the second Most Powerful Actress on the Planet – beating many more far more established actresses including the likes of Angelina Jolie to the top spot. She is now the second highest paid actress in

Hollywood, just behind Sandra Bullock, whose career began two decades earlier.

Jennifer is also due to appear in the *Guinness World Records* for having scooped so many awards in such a short space of time.

And so, the question is, what next for the girl who went from a seemingly disastrous fashion photo shoot for *Abercrombie & Fitch* to a handful of little-known indie films to being known around the globe as the *Girl on Fire* in the most successful franchise of all time?

She has hinted that she would love to work behind the cameras: 'I've always wanted to direct,' she told *Vanity Fair*. 'Ever since *The Poker House*. Lori Petty was directing and I was imagining being a director. I love filmmaking. I love acting, but I don't feel married to being in front of the camera.'

Jennifer is already signed on to produce a few films, but before all that all she really wants is a break from her hectic schedule, which has seen her work back to back since she first found fame in 2008.

'I want my life as normal as possible,' she has said. 'One of the dangers in the film industry is that things are too fast, aging. I do not want to burn the stages of my life.'

And with the coming years mapped out for her, it is hardly surprising that Jennifer said she would love to take a well-earned break from filming to get a rest, but with so many projects in the pipeline, it is unclear when this may come.

In some of her more revealing interviews, Jennifer has wistfully suggested that all she really longs for is to buy a house where she can actually spend more than a few days at a time and disappear off the radar. Being so instantly recognisable, the one thing she craves is anonymity and privacy; her dream is to simply vanish far from the intense glare of the public eye.

Until now she has managed to keep her feet firmly on the ground, in a refreshingly honest and candid way, but the demands on her time are relentless. She has said she misses being able to relax on the sofa, watching her beloved reality TV shows, and the freedom to ride horses as she did as a child.

Luckily she is surrounded by the strong bonds of her loving family, who do their best to ensure that she returns as often as possible to her childhood home where she can enjoy some peace and normality.

It was not so very long ago that she was enduring regular therapy sessions to tackle her crippling social anxieties and emotional disorders, so many would say time away from the intense grind of the Hollywood machine is essential before she breaks down, just as so many big name stars have done before her.

Paparazzi photographers and eager fans with camera phones hound Jennifer relentlessly and aggressively. Gossip columnists, magazine and TV shows speculate and dissect every dress she wears, every man she is seen with, and indeed every move she makes. She admits she does not feel at home in Los Angeles: one false step and it could all come crashing down around her.

Indeed she has said: 'Louisville is actually really respectful. I can normally go out to dinner with my family and everybody is really nice about letting me have a nice experience. The only thing I'll ever identify with as home is Louisville.'

She may still feel like the girl next door, but one thing is certain – Jennifer Lawrence is Hollywood royalty and as long as she continues to tread carefully, she seems destined to reign over her kingdom for many years to come.